P9-DCM-415

cattle Drive

By

Debby Schoeningh

To Marcia!
Happy Cow
Trails!
Debby Schoeningh

The Country
Side Press

Copyright © 2009 Debby Schoeningh, The Country Side Press

All Rights Reserved. No part of the material protected by this copyright notice may be reproduced in any form or by any electronic or mechanical means without written permission from the author/publisher.

Some of the stories in this book contain fictitious names. Any resemblance of these characters to real people you know, is purely coincidental. Any resemblance of these characters to people you don't know, doesn't matter so don't have a cow, man.

A few people were trampled, butted and kicked, but no cows were harmed in the making of this book.

Library of Congress Control Number: 2009912410

ISBN Number: 0-9746360-2-9   978-0-9746360-2-3

Published by The Country Side Press
49850 Miller Road
North Powder, OR 97867

Front and Back cover designs by Margie Brown
Edited by Eloise Dielman
Printed in USA by Lightning Source

Dedications

To those who dedicate their lives to being good stewards of the land, preserving what God has entrusted to them with respect for wildlife and future generations to come.

To my husband, Mike, my soul mate, my teacher, my best friend, and the one who still makes me giggle like a schoolgirl after all these years.

To my son, Jake, whose kindness, compassion and perseverance make me proud, and whose zest for life keeps me young.

To my mom and dad, and brother, Tom, whose confidence in me has inspired me to pursue my dreams.

To Pete and Donna who have given us a great opportunity to live, ranch and play in the most beautiful place on earth.

Acknowledgements

Special thanks to Eloise Dielman for editing <u>Cattle Drive</u>, to Margie Brown for her wonderful artwork on the front and back cover, and to all of my family and friends for their encouragement.

Painting by Naomi Schoeningh

Contents

Cattle Drive

Having been a rancher now for 20 years I'd almost forgotten what it feels like to be a city slicker and not know the difference between heifers, cows, steers and bulls. I can remember calling them all "cows" regardless of their gender or age before I became one of the enlightened ones myself.

As hard as it was for me to learn the ways of a rancher, I've found it can be even more difficult for a foreigner to comprehend.

My friend and neighbor, Glenda, recently had an online chat with a woman named Sharon who lived in England. They had agreed on a time to meet for the chat and Glenda was running a little late.

Their conversation went something like this:

Glenda: "Sorry I'm late, I got slowed down by a cattle drive."

Sharon: "Cattle drive?"

Glenda: "Yes."

Sharon: "Are you serious?"

Glenda: "Of course I am. I wouldn't make that up!"

Sharon: "I had no idea that cattle drive. Where do they drive?"

Glenda: "Usually right down the highway, but sometimes they go down the gravel roads around here, too."

Sharon: "Amazing! How fast do they drive?"

Glenda: "About five miles per hour unless they get excited. Then they go a little faster."

Sharon: "Excited?"

Glenda: "Yeah, you know if a dog chases them or somebody honks their horn, they tend to get a little worked up."

Sharon: "So let me get this straight. Cattle drive about five miles per hour down the highway… would that be in the left or right lane?"

Glenda: "They usually go down the middle of the road. That's why I was late; it takes awhile to find an opening to get around them."

Sharon: "So how many cattle do this driving thing anyway?"

Glenda: "Oh, around here usually a couple hundred head at a time. But in some really big drives there can be a 1,000 or more."

Sharon: "Now I know you are pulling my leg. I can almost believe one or two could manage it with some kind of special devices, but if there were 1,000 cattle driving down the road anywhere in the world, even though I live in England, I think I would have heard about it. That would be in the news everywhere."

Glenda, getting impatient with her friend's skepticism: "O.K. Missy, just how do they move cattle from one field to another where you live?"

Sharon: "Simple, the cattle walk."

Glenda: "So what's the difference? I told you they go pretty slow here, too, unless they get excited."

Sharon: "Yeah, but in England cattle don't know how to drive, and I for one wouldn't want a cow stuffing herself behind the wheel of my BMW with her little kiddies hanging their hooves out the back windows!"

Glenda: "Oh, for goodness sake, the cattle here don't drive cars. They are *driven* down the road."

Sharon: "Oh, well, that explains a lot. Do they have to sit in the back or do they get to ride in the front passenger seat?"

Glenda: "Once and for all cattle do not drive, they do not ride in any type of car as a passenger or otherwise — they are pushed down the road by cowboys on horses."

Sharon: "Now you're telling me bulls can ride horses?"

Glenda: "What?'

Sharon: "Isn't that what a cow 'boy' is — a bull?"

Glenda, not wanting to continue this conversation: "You know, you're right. I was just kidding about the whole cattle drive thing. I was really late because my dog ate my computer mouse and I had to make him cough it up."

Sharon: "Well why didn't you just say so to begin with? You could have saved me from getting my knickers in a twist."

Glenda: "You wear knickers?"

Sharon: "Why of course, don't you?"

Glenda: "No."

Sharon: "Good Heavens, no respectable woman would go out in public without her knickers!"

Glenda: "Nobody here wears knickers — except maybe golfers. What's the big deal?"

Sharon: "You Americans must not have any modesty whatsoever!"

Glenda, sensing there must be something amiss, did a quick Internet search. *Knickers: in England the word for women's undergarments, i.e. panties.* She quickly resumed her online chat: "Oh, yes, I do wear knickers!"

Sharon: "And I suppose now you're going to tell me that cattle really can drive?

There comes a moment in every online chat when you instinctively know it's time to sign off. For Glenda, that time had come.

Calf Butt Patrol or Oh, Yeah, I Meant to Tell You

Calving is finally over, but now the diarrhea season is upon us. Every day we walk through the cows and check their youngsters for signs of coccidiosis, an illness they get from drinking out of contaminated puddles of water. They have fresh running water just steps away from them at all times, but invariably they go out of their way, crossing fences, mountains the size of Everest and swimming rivers with white water rapids to find a dirty puddle to drink out of.

I think the cows put them up to it as part of their ninja kicking training or something. "My son, in order to see the great white calf, you must first drink from the puddle of knowledge, then all good things will come to you, including the runs."

At any rate, early detection and treatment of this disease is crucial so we patrol the herd daily looking at messy rear ends like Sherlock Holmes after his arch nemesis. Once you spot a calf with the afore mentioned posterior condition, you have to determine if it is indeed coccidiosis or just a calf that has imbibed in too much milk. The only sure way to tell is to watch it "in action."

Some people call their spouses and say, "Guess what, honey, I just got a promotion and a raise!" Ranchers call their spouses and say, "Guess what, honey, the calf just pooped and it looks normal!"

Once you do find a calf, however, that has coccidiosis, treatment is very difficult, not because giving it an antibiotic shot and sulfa pills is hard, but because you have to catch it first!

A two-month old calf with coccidiosis may look and act sick, as if it has no energy and is just barely dragging itself around the field, but get hold of it and it will be dragging you around.

Last week there was a calf in the herd that was so miserable it was walking like its rear end was competing with its head for the lead position. My husband, Mike, tiptoed up behind it and grabbed the calf by the back leg with a 10-foot pole with a hook on the end. The calf, that only moments before would have qualified as a poster child for sloth-like behavior, immediately came to life and started running.

I grabbed onto the pole behind Mike in an attempt to help slow it down, but only succeeded in letting it drag both of us around the field. We must have looked like we were playing an old schoolyard game of crack the whip as the calf zigzagged us back and forth across the pasture thrashing me around at the end of a pole.

In all the commotion Mike somehow managed to slip a rope around the calf's foot. With me manning the pole and him the rope we got the calf in a different gear – reverse – and pulled him over to the four-wheeler. Mike instructed me to keep holding onto the calf with the pole while he tried to tie the rope off to the four-wheeler.

While I was still wrestling with the calf on the end of the pole, Mike with his back to me said, "I meant to tell you whatever you do don't get between the calf and the four-wheeler."

"Too late," I croaked as he turned to find me sprawled across the four-wheeler on my back with my legs strapped to it like a damsel in distress on the railroad tracks.

My hero maneuvered the calf back around the four-wheeler to release the rope that bound me, but before I could get upright and off my back the calf, still tied, took off on three legs dragging the four-wheeler.

"Oh yeah, I meant to tell you to put the Honda in gear," Mike called after me.

While going at an incredible speed I somehow managed to roll over on my stomach, inch my way up to the seat without falling off and put the brakes on. I felt like a stagecoach driver jumping onto a horse's back to save the passengers from a runaway team. Well… O.K., the calf was probably only pulling it at about 10 yards per hour, but still, I could have fallen off and been seriously injured and the calf might have run through a fence or worse yet into a cow and made her mad before I got it stopped.

We finally got the calf doctored and as Mike took the rope off of its hind leg it stood quietly.

No sooner than I said, "Well, it looks like the calf finally decided we weren't the enemy after all," it reared up on its front legs and planted a well-placed kick to my thigh before bounding off to join the herd.

"I meant to tell you to watch out for the calf; it might kick," said Mike. "By the way what's for dinner?"

"Oh, yeah, I meant to tell you," I said. "We're going out for dinner…"

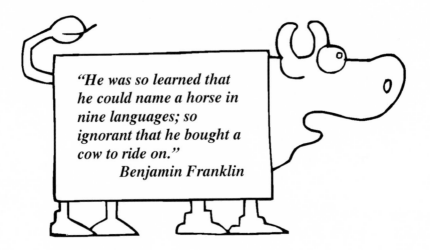

"He was so learned that he could name a horse in nine languages; so ignorant that he bought a cow to ride on."
Benjamin Franklin

Plastic Earrings - All The Rage In Calf Accessories

There are several advantages to ear tagging calves. It helps identify which cow they came out of, gives you an easy way to record which calves have been doctored, and makes it easier to pick one out of a crowd, especially when they all look alike. You can say, "Oh, look at number 34; isn't he cute?"

rather than having to say, "Oh, look at the one 40 feet from the 14th fence post on the south side of the pasture standing parallel to the barn with his mom who is the same color as the rest of the cows and has no unusual markings to make her stand out from the herd. Isn't he... oh, never mind, he moved."

Ear tagging gives a cow or calf an identity. And since most cows can't use the computer or answer the phone, it is very difficult to steal a cow's identity. Occasionally they lose their identity because it falls out, but the only way a cow can steal another cow's identity is to step on it. And since most cows have two ear tags, they still retain at least half of their identity.

Even with all of these advantages, though, there is one big disadvantage to ear tagging calves — getting the tags in their ears. Contrary to people, who actually pay someone to poke holes in their ears, noses, belly buttons and other various body parts, calves don't seem to like it much. They run as fast as they can when they see us coming with the ear tagger. In fact, when you try to explain to them that plastic earrings are all the rage in calf accessories, they seem to understand the "rage" part, but little else.

Ear taggers work like a pair of pliers, just one quick squeeze of the handles and it's over. We're not asking them to stay still while we numb their ears with ice cubes, place a potato behind it and poke a hole through with a large sewing needle. It's a very quick process, and would take less than two seconds if they would just cooperate.

We had one calf the other day that my husband, Mike, walked up behind and grabbed the hind foot with a calf catch. A calf catch is a long aluminum pole with a hook on the end that allows you to catch a critter from about 10 feet away. Needless to stay the calf didn't like the idea much and was well on his way to trying out for bucking rodeo stock.

Mike had inched his hands down the pole to within about three feet of the critter, but couldn't get hold of the thrashing calf. He yelled to me to grab the end of the pole behind him to hold the calf's foot so he could let go long enough to grab the calf by the head. I soon discovered that grabbing the end of a long pole that is moving up and down

10

and sideways, flaying uncontrollably as the calf hops around on three legs, is harder than it looks. That pole nearly beat me senseless about the head. I was close to developing cauliflower ears like the professional boxers do from getting hit too many times before I finally managed to get hold of it. Once I finally did latch onto it, it became pretty apparent — probably by the sight of me being drug around the field at the end of a 10 feet pole by the adrenaline high calf — that I wasn't going to be able to hold it for long.

Mike chased us down and threw his arms around the calf's neck and we came to a screeching halt.

"O.K.," he said, "Drop the pole and come up here and hold the calf so I can tag it."

I let go of the bar, which gave me a parting whack on the back of the head, and did as I was instructed.

I wrapped my arms around the calf's neck putting my whole body into it and waited… nothing happened.

"How do you expect me to tag him if you have his ears covered?" Mike said.

So I straddled the calf between my legs and hung on around its chest — that didn't work. The squirming calf almost got away.

The calf and I wrestled around some more until we finally fell to the ground. I soon found out that calves can kick almost as hard lying on their sides as they can standing up. As I was fending off the thrashing hooves like a seasoned Kung Fu fighter, I felt the hot breath of a mad cow sniffing my backside. Before I had a chance to wonder if the cow was going to flatten me, one of the calf's flaying hooves hit her on the nose. The cow shook her head and snorted before going back to a nearby pile of hay to commiserate with the other cows about how her own kid socked her in the snout.

I knew how she felt; I had about had it with her kid too.

But Mike reminded me that if I kept messing around the calf would get away and we would never be able to catch it again.

So with my last ounce of strength I threw my body on the calf and pinned it to the ground. All those years of watching Saturday Night Wrestling finally paid off. Mike waded through the panting heap of tangled legs, arms and hooves, until he finally managed to find the calf's ears and tag them.

I let the calf up and rather than running, he just stood there next to me leaning against my legs. After all that fussing and fighting to try and get out of having his ears tagged, I couldn't figure out why he didn't take off. Then I looked over at the herd and there stood his mother shaking her head and bellowing at him. In cow language I'm pretty sure she was saying something like, "You get over here, young man, right this minute!" Only now she could call him by his full name, "Number Fourteen." When mom calls you by your full name that always translates to "You're in big trouble now!"

Poo Posies At
The Museum of Ag

Museums of Agriculture have popped up all over the country in the last decade or so. It's nice that Americans are interested in our line of work, but I don't understand why people need to pay to go into one of these museums when they could drive through the countryside and see many of those same exhibits for free.

Every rancher has a junk pile... er... ah... I mean spare parts warehouse with oodles of antiques. Wanna see the tracks from a 1929 Caterpillar up close? How about a 1910 John Deere walking plow? When it was no longer needed, the farmer walked it right over to the pile and gave it one last shove.

A complete Reeves threshing machine could probably be put back together if you had time to sort through the pile for parts.

More often than not you won't, however, find that 1921 McCormick-Deering tractor in the pile because they are still in use. In fact, a lot of antique ranchers and farmers are still in use too.

One thing that is not very realistic about the Ag museum displays is that they show the farming equipment with shiny paint and polished chrome. How many farmers and ranchers do you know who wash and wax their tractors or buff their balers? The museum could at least let the dust settle on them and leave the seat ripped for authenticity.

A real advantage we ranchers have over museums is that you get to see the items in their natural habitat instead of a manufactured setting with a painted sunrise. The fields are littered with old hay derricks that sit right where they loaded the last horse drawn wagon.

Manure spreaders can be found in front yards everywhere in the country. City folks naturally think these items are yard ornaments because they have flowers growing out of them. But in reality it doesn't take long for livestock poo left in the spreader to grow a crop of wild posies in between uses. Along those lines, I'm surprised that museums don't have fossilized rancher's footprints on display because everywhere they step, they leave a trail of poo that fertilizes the ground and stains the kitchen linoleum.

Some of the museums boast that you can see wood with the nails still intact retrieved from a 100 year-old barn. Heck, you can drive through the countryside just about anywhere now and see the whole flipping barn still in use.

The museum exhibits with manikins are what really intrigue me though.

One museum has a display with an old guy sitting on the porch staring off into the distance with a bottle of moonshine next to him with the title "Just Sitting and Ruminating." Just replace the moonshine with a six-pack of

Bud and we have our own little museum exhibit right here almost every night.

Another shows a woman slaving away in the kitchen over a hot stove while her husband relaxes with his stocking feet propped up on the table. I don't think you need to delve into history to see that – it's still a pretty common occurrence.

A universal feature of many of the museums is to try your hand at some everyday farm chores. Shoot, I don't know of many farmers and ranchers who wouldn't let you try your hand at bucking bales, branding calves, digging fence posts and chopping thistles for real, and they wouldn't charge you anything to do it.

One Museum boasts that you can journey back to a time "when farmers and ranchers used muscle power." What do they think we use now – flab power? I noticed there wasn't any mention of us using brainpower for anything. Whether or not that is an intentional oversight, I don't know….

While searching online I ran across one exhibit called the "Museum of irrigated agriculture." To its credit, it appeared to have more than just a shovel on display. But to be realistic they would have to show ditches with sod and rocks piled at strategic points to divert water onto a rancher's pasture. There would then need to be a county watermaster looking at the situation, and the rancher with a sign over his head with the words, "Dang, how did that get there?"

Most of the museums have what they call "miniature farm" displays. With the economy going the way it is we all have "miniature" farms now. That's not old; it's new.

If they are going to have authentic museums of Ag, though, there are a few exhibits I would like to see.

How about one that shows the transition from when contented cows became mad cows. I would suspect it happened about 1860 the same time the first milking machine was invented. The first machines had continuous suction like a vacuum cleaner that were powerful enough to suck a Volkswagen through a garden hose.

I'd like to see an exhibit that shows how farmers have recycled baling twine over the years — from the bale to the tractor muffler to the dog leash to a pair of five button Levi's. The title could be something like "Baling twine is a man's Midol." I might add, they would need to display a giant pile of twine to be historically accurate, and I would be willing to donate ours for such a good cause.

Another good display would be how rancher's wives have gone from working in the fields in Carhart overalls like hired hands to running the business in expensive designer suits, and making all of the important decisions. Technically that's not history, though. Maybe it would be better suited for a museum of the near future.

When my husband heard of this exhibit I had to remind him that there is no such thing as a museum of ranch wives with vivid imaginations. I am thinking, however, that there should be a museum of the different kinds of couches men have had to sleep on throughout history.

In the meantime, if you are so inclined and feel it would be a more rewarding experience if you had to pay for an Ag museum tour, then yes, by all means, please give us money. Whenever you see a piece of antique equipment sitting in a field, just put cash or check in an envelope and drop it off in the nearest mailbox. Or knock on the door of the nearest farmhouse — most of us accept Visa and MasterCard.

Hackin' and Whackin'
The Bristled Thistle

Thistles are a rancher's proverbial thorn in the side, and in the finger, and occasionally the ankle and sometimes the butt…The son of a biscuits are everywhere and multiply faster than zucchini on a hot day.

I've taken down a thistle or two or three during my years on the ranch, but this is the first year I've been placed on thistle patrol. As such I am a Private First Class of the

Broadleaf Battalion and my husband is my self-appointed Commander in Chief. The only privileges a Private First Class gets on our ranch is a break for lunch, because the Private has to make it for the Commander, and a new shovel.

When he first ordered, I mean asked, me to accept this weed fraught mission, I had reservations, but the lure of that shiny new shovel was just too tempting. He dangled it in front of me with the sharpened blade gleaming like he was enticing me with a diamond necklace.

"See how pretty and shiny it is," he said. "It will be all yours and no one else will be able to use it."

Wow, my very own shovel! I was so excited I had to go in the house and contemplate this new development while scrubbing the toilet, coincidently with my very own brush, which no one else is apparently able to use either.

I decided the exercise would do me good and after all how hard could it be to chop down a few thistles? I emerged from the house a short time later ready to thump on some thistles, but my shiny new shovel that had been ceremoniously propped up against the porch by my Commander was no where to be found.

I searched around the yard, in the shop, next to the driveway and couldn't find it anywhere. I was just about to give up when the Commander pulled into the driveway.

"I can't find my new shovel," I said as he stepped out of the pickup.

"Oh, I think I may have seen it down by the barn," he said somewhat reluctantly.

I started off to the barn, but remembered that I had left my gloves in the pickup earlier that day so turned back just in time to see the Commander dragging my shiny new shovel out from under a pile of irrigation tarps in the back of the pickup.

"By golly, look what I found," he said feigning surprise when he saw me approach. "I wonder how it got in there?"

I stood before him with my arms crossed giving him the ranch wife's eye, a kind of half squinted sideways look that we normally develop within the first year of marriage.

"Oh, my gosh," I said rather sarcastically as I grabbed the shovel, "it must have taken a flying leap right out of your hands and into the truck."

"Yeah, imagine that," he grinned.

I headed out for the nearest thistle, while glaring at him, but since it's hard to walk and give the ranch wife's eye at the same time, I eventually had to let it go or fall on my face.

"Make sure you get those in the far pasture next to the road when you're through up here," he called after me.

Puddin' Head, our black lab, Lord only knows what cross, was bouncing around with me as I became a human weed whacker. After about 40 minutes I had eradicated every thistle within a 100-yard radius of the yard fence and decided that this wasn't too bad a job after all. "Why does everyone make such a big deal of hackin' and whackin' a few thistles?" I wondered.

"Well, Puddin'," I said looking at my watch, "if we hurry and get those down by the road, we'll make it back just in time to watch Oprah." Puddin' always gets excited about watching Oprah. I don't like to watch it myself, of course; I just like to keep the dog happy.

As we approached the pasture near the road, I could hardly believe my eyes. In sharp contrast to the three or four dozen thistles we had just chopped down in the upper pasture, there were bazillions of them here! "Alrighty, so this is why thistles are such a big deal," I told Puddin'.

Scattered along the hillside like an invading army they stood waving in the breeze taunting me. Puddin' and I were completely outnumbered even with a new shovel.

"This will take forever," I told Puddin'.

She looked up at me whining sympathetically.

"Oh well," I said to her, "it's not like Oprah even has a last name; I guess this is more important."

I pried, pummeled and puckered thistle after thistle. I became one with the shovel, literally. I had gripped the shovel so long and so hard that my hands wouldn't un-grip to let go of it. What seemed like forever, actually it was about 30 minutes and a sock full of stickers later, I decided it was time to call for reinforcements.

I whipped out my cell phone and called the Commander.

"Have you seen how many thistles are down here?" I said. "There's no way I can chop all of these down before they go to seed."

"Are you sure you're not just wanting to go watch Oprah?" he asked.

"No, good grief!" I said. "There's just too many of them. Couldn't I cut them down with the swather or something?"

"Well, there is one thing," he said, "that might be a little easier — chemical warfare."

"You mean…" I started to ask.

"Yes," he interrupted, "2, 4-D. But you will still have to get the big ones with a shovel. They don't respond as well to 2, 4-D as the little ones."

"Just how big is big?" I asked.

"Anything over about 16 inches," he replied.

After a quick survey of the area, I determined that everything was under 16 inches. Of course I didn't have a ruler on me, but heck I knew they were at least all under three feet and that seemed close enough — give or take a couple of inches.

So I returned to the base and came back outfitted with a four-wheeler and a tank full of chemical. Puddin' got to stay home this time to avoid getting sprayed — lucky dog got to watch Oprah after all.

I rode through the weeds astride the four-wheeler like a cowgirl in a western movie shooting vermin thistle on all sides with a 2,4-D spray gun. The bristled thistle began to recoil. If they had legs they would have run for their lives because they were no match for me and my chemical equipped Honda.

Even with this time saving technique, it was still three hours later when I pulled up in the driveway weary from battle.

I informed the commander that I had the enemy on the run and they were wilting fast.

He said, "Good job, Private. Tomorrow you can go back and chop down the big ones with a shovel."

"But..." I started to protest until he gave me the rancher's eye, which is similar to the ranch wife's eye, only really not fair at all.

"O.K.," I conceded, but first there is something I have to do."

What's that?" he said.

"I need to go get some spray paint so I can give my shovel a pink handle so no one else will be tempted to use it."

A rancher/ranch wife's eye stare off ensued...

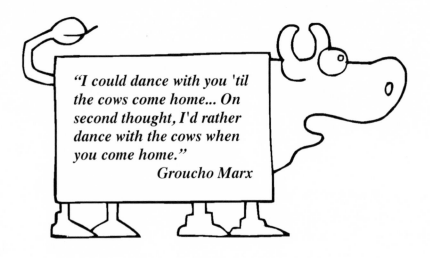

"I could dance with you 'til the cows come home... On second thought, I'd rather dance with the cows when you come home."

Groucho Marx

Dial 1-800-Bad-Calf

We don't talk about it much, but nine out of 10 ranch wives are physically abused. I know those numbers are shocking, but I suspect it is even higher than that. The 10th woman is either abused and not fessing up or is still on her honeymoon and hasn't had to run calves up the chute yet.

We try not to complain, we always hope the next time it will be different, that the calves will somehow see the error in their ways and go calmly up the chute without kicking and stomping and head butting the heck out of us. But it is never different....

My neighbor, Bev, says that abuse by calves has gotten so bad on their ranch that she has to wear dark pantyhose to hide the bruises on her legs when she wears a dress. And just about the time the bruises heal, it's time to wrestle another calf up the chute.

Most of us have tried many different tactics to stop the abuse. I've found one way to avoid being kicked by a calf is to stand as close to its rear end as possible. That way the calf doesn't have enough room to wind up for a really hard kick. This however, presents another problem – next to a calf's rear end is not a pleasant place to be. Just about the time I think I've escaped being kicked, the calf will poop. This of course causes me to jump back to avoid getting splattered and gives the calf the distance it needs to wind up and kick me square in the shin. Ranch wives commonly refer to this as the old "poop and punt" trick.

Calves have another trick, which they perform often, where they run past you at full speed and give you a little sideways kick. We call this the dash and poop because let's face it, they are always pooping. This doesn't hurt as much as the full contact kick you get standing behind them, but it's enough of an impact to cause a bruise.

Even if by some miracle we avoid getting kicked hard while working calves, the largest calf in the herd inevitably decides to practice the Flamingo dance on our feet. It can't be satisfied with just a few little stomps. It has to perform the entire dance routine — the only thing missing is the guitar player and the castanets. Thus, and rightly so, this is referred to as the "poop and prance."

One thing I learned early on is to never bend over around a calf. They interpret your available backside as an invitation to practice their head butting skills. One time after being kicked by a calf in the chute, I bent over to rub my shin and the calf behind me butted me. It wasn't too hard, but it threw me off balance enough that I hit my head on the side of the chute and fell getting covered in mud and Lord only knows what else.

Which reminds me, the safety equipment industry has completely neglected ranch wives. I have never seen a helmet, padded clothing, special boots or any kind of strap or guard made for ranch wives who push calves up the chute. However, give a man a football, baseball or a hockey puck, and a multi-million dollar protective gear manufacturing business is born.

Due to the lack of support offered ranch wives in situations when they are exposed to abuse by a calf, I've often thought of starting a hotline, 1-800-bad-calf. Ranch wives could call to get the straight poop on what to do when they are a victim of abusive calves.

Caller: "Hello, bad calf hotline? I just can't take it any more. One calf kicked me five times today before I managed to get him in the head catch. To make matters worse, I have to work calves again today and I have to go to a dinner party tomorrow tonight and would like to wear a dress. Is there anyway to avoid getting kicked again so my legs aren't completely black and blue?"

Bad Calf: "I see your problem, but unfortunately, there is no way to prevent calves from being abusive at this time. I would suggest that you call Bev and ask her where she buys her bruise concealing pantyhose."

"*Sacred cows make the best hamburger.*"
Mark Twain

The Weaning

We weaned our calves last week and are still suffering from calf lag, which is similar to jet lag, but you don't get to go anywhere.

Over the years we have tried separating the calves from the cows first thing in the morning in hopes that by nightfall they would be settled down a little. We've also tried separating them late in the day in hopes that they wouldn't get too upset until the next day. But it doesn't seem to matter much because inevitably they decide the best time to really let loose and complain is just as we are about to fall asleep.

This year I even tried reasoning with our cows and calves. I told the cows to look at the bright side: their kids were out of the pasture, no more cleaning up after them, no more round the clock feedings, and they no longer had to find a babysitter when they wanted to go off into the far corners of the field to be alone.

I talked to the calves and told them they were now free to do anything they wanted without being reprimanded by their parent. They could stay up late, sleep in late, eat grass until they were bloated and butt heads to their heart's content. Heck, I even told them now that they were weaned they could get a tattoo branded on their sides and their ears pierced with square tags just like the adults.

Needless to say the calves weren't very responsive. They just stood there and looked at me like I was flapping my jaws in the wind and making nonsensical noises, similar to my own son, who by the way does not get the same branding and tattooing privileges.

The weaning always starts off slow with a couple of calves bawling, which in turn gets a few cows bellowing and before long the whole herd is engaged in a pasture-wide moo-a-thon. There are times in the middle of the night when they give up for a few moments, but they have a backup system. During those momentary lapses as they rest their moo-chords, the cows have apparently entered into an agreement with the elk to ensure that we don't get any sleep. (Come to think of it this agreement is probably why the cows allow the elk to come in and eat our pastures forcing us to buy more hay — if you'll help us make noise all night for a week, we'll let you have the best clover.)

The minute our cows stop mooing, the cow elk start squealing on cue almost as if there is a bovine maestro waving a baton at the different animal orchestra sections to let them know when to start and how loud to wail. I suspect that while the elk are squealing, our cows are all standing around the water trough wetting their whistles and practicing their moo scales (moo, ray, me) preparing for their next musical set of the Cowharmonic led by Maestro Angus No. 43.

I've tried to tone down the elk section some during weaning nights by banging two pan lids together, but apparently the orchestra is not in need of a pajama clad cymbal ensemble as they pretty much ignore me.

After a few fitful hours of wrapping pillows around our ears and tossing and turning trying to sleep through the noise, there is at least somewhat of a reprieve. The cows stop mooing, the calves stop bawling and the elk stop squealing all at the same time. This is only however because the Maestro waves his baton at the soprano section — the coyotes. Once they start howling, our dog, Puddin' Head, recognizes her cue in this a Cappella musical and performs a solo from the front porch.

Finally on about the fifth night at about 2 a.m., the all-animal orchestra, which by then has included a few guest appearances in the form of caterwauling felines, comes to an end. And then, I bolt upright in bed, "What's that?" I ask my husband who was also stirred from his sleep aided by my kicking him in the shins.

"I don't know," he says as we both strain our ears in the darkness to hear. There's nothing... it's absolutely silent for the first time in almost a week. Yet we keep straining to hear this nothing that woke us up as if it were in itself a noise....

After a few minutes a little sound begins to pierce the darkness. As it begins to grow louder and louder we recognize it as our old friend the croaking toad who sits below our bedroom window crooning on cool fall nights.

"Whew," I let out a sigh of relief. "For a minute there I thought it was quiet."

"Yeah, that was kind of creepy," he says.

"When a cow endeavors to scratch her ear, it means a rain shower is very near. When she thumps her ribs with an angry tail, look out for thunder, lightning and hail."   *Proverb*

Smacking the Bulls
in the Hood

I've finally figured out why bulls are called "bulls" – it's because they are bullies. They are always picking on some cow (no wonder cows get so mad), someone, something or each other. If bulls were allowed in the schoolyards, they would be the ones shaking you down every day for your lunch money and giving you wedgies.

We have one bull that is about four years old, and he has been ruler of the pastures this year because of his large size. Our 2-year old bulls have tried to take him on, but it's like watching a Volkswagen Beetle collide with a Hummer – you know which one is going to stay on the road and which one is going to get shoved into the ditch before it even happens.

The reign of power shifted this week when the older bull ended up lame. We don't have any idea how it happened, but he somehow injured his shoulder and can barely walk. The 2-year olds took advantage of his weakness and formed an alliance like some kind of Bulls in the Hood gang, and together beat up on the older bull. The older bull stood his ground, but after each encounter, and there were several a day, it was obvious his shoulder was getting worse.

This presented a problem because the older bull was too far out in the pasture to get him to a corral because he could barely stand, much less walk, and it was obvious he couldn't or wouldn't climb into a livestock trailer without a great deal of assistance.

My husband and I discussed several ways to get him out of the pasture and away from the Bulls in the Hood including haltering him and hooking a come-along to it to ratchet him up a makeshift ramp into the trailer. We thought I could also give him a little incentive from behind by pushing his butt with my Subaru. We discounted that idea though because similar to an age-old riddle, "Where does a 2,000-pound bull sit?" Anywhere he wants to — and in this case it would probably be on the hood of my Subaru.

Short of hiring a helicopter to lift him or hoisting him onto a flatbed with a crane, we finally decided the best plan of action would be to leave him where he is and build an electric fence around him to the keep the young bulls out. "Brilliant idea!" you say. Yes, we thought so, but there was still the problem of keeping the Bulls in the Hood away from him while we erected the fence, which would take several hours.

Since the National Guard would probably think defending the country was a little more important than defending our bull, we decided my husband would put up the fence while I became the bull's bodyguard.

I armed myself with my weapon of choice, a shovel, mainly because I always seem to have one in my hands anyway, and stood by the bull's side waiting for the attack from the Hood. It didn't take long.

Just as I was in mid chorus of "Bad bulls, bad bulls, whatcha gonna do..." two young bulls came charging across the pasture bellowing some kind of bovine war cry and skidded to a stop about 20 feet away. They proceeded toward the big guy and me with a kind of lopsided shoulder first, head down walk that was their way of showing they meant business. Again, if they had been bullies in the schoolyard, they would have been punching their fists into their open hand to try to intimidate us.

I stepped in front of the old bull, raised my shovel and gave my best "Cowabunga" yell. The two young bulls turned and ran.

"See, it's just that easy," I said to the old bull that in return snorted at me. Unfortunately, the young bulls interpreted that snort as a challenge and came galloping back.

"Now look what you've done," I told the old bull. He just blinked his eyes and shrugged his good shoulder as he braced himself for a fight.

This time the two were not buying my Cowabunga routine and did not retreat. I hopped up and down, called them names and told them I'd tell their rancher on them, but they kept advancing. One of them lowered his head and tried to get around me to the old bull so I smacked him square on the forehead with the flat side of the shovel. He spun around bucking and running, fortunately away from me, and bellowing.

In the meantime, the other bull had tried to attack the old bull from behind so I turned and smacked him on the head as well. They both ran off to soothe their injured egos and stood a short distance away, looking at me as if to say, "How could you?"

This repeated charging, shovel smacking, and retreating went on for over an hour.

I finally yelled over to my husband, "If I'm going to have to keep this up much longer, I'll need a cape, red boots and gold wristbands." He turned and flashed a big grin at me. "No," I said, "I was just kidding. I'm not going to dress up like Wonder Woman for you."

Now would be a good time to point out that my husband was less than 20 yards away during all of this. I probably wouldn't have hit a bull on the head with anything without knowing I could run over and stand behind him if one of the bulls were to become incensed at my shovel smacking and retaliate. You always need to have a good buffer handy — or at the very least someone you can run faster than — when you start smacking bulls.

The old bull soon tired of standing. I'm not sure why, because it's not like he had to actually do anything during this whole ordeal, but he decided to lie down. As soon as he stretched out on the ground the two young bulls meandered back out into the pasture to graze with the rest of the herd.

"That's it," I said to the old bull. "All you have to do is lie down and they go away? Couldn't you have thought of that a little sooner?" After all I had done to protect him he just closed his eyes and sighed like I was a pesky, noisy little fly on his backside.

Sledding Calf and the Creature from the Swamp

Calving in two feet of snow has been a challenge this year, especially for our first time heifers. They seem to have the natural instinct that tells them to seek out a somewhat secluded location to give birth to their four-legged bundles of joy, but I don't think calving on the side of an icy hill is what the creator had in mind.

Somewhere along their neurotransmitter lines, the message starts out as "find a suitable location" and ends up something like "just park it anywhere, sister." The highest snowdrift, the slickest slab of ice or the deepest irrigation ditch they can find are apparently all within their realm of great places to have a baby.

To top it off they cross their legs and hold on to that baby until they sense an impending blizzard and then wait until the snow and wind are at their peak. I think they also stick a hoof in their mouths and hold it up to check the direction of the wind and make sure they position themselves so it is blowing directly on the emerging calf.

We had one heifer that tried in earnest to calve on a 20-foot glacier and finally gave up. My husband, Mike, and I herded her to the barn and tried to get her into a nice clean stall that we had prepared with straw bedding. No amount of coaxing or pushing could convince her to go into the stall. Instead she lay down in the barn's alleyway and plopped her offspring onto the dirt floor.

Once the wet, slimy calf came to life it started flopping around in the dirt and as it tried to stand up, it looked like some creature rising from the swamp in a horror movie. The heifer took one look at the mud-caked youngster and ran into the stall, the stall that only moments before we couldn't make her go in to.

Since it was obvious the heifer wasn't going to get much accomplished on her own, I began cleaning off and drying the calf while Mike went to check the other heifers. By this time it was midnight, the snow was blowing and the wind was howling.

Another heifer had calved in the field on a pile of snow and the calf had gotten too cold and couldn't get up. We brought it into the house and dried it off with hair dryers and electric heaters, but it was too weak to stand. We decided to leave it under the pile of blankets next to the stove and go lay down on the couch and get some sleep.

At 2 a.m., we are really not at our best and having each other's feet in our faces as we struggled to get comfortable in our insulated Carhartts didn't help much. The first hour was taken up with complaints like "you're kneeing me in the back," "you're laying on my elbow," and "get your toe out of my nose." In spite of this we somehow managed to drift off to sleep anyway.

Just as I was getting used to the smell of wool socks that had spent the last 12 hours sweating in a pair of Sorrell snow boots the sun rose over the couch and it was time to get up. We got the calf up, managed to get a little milk down him and then took him outside to find his mother.

You've probably heard the saying, "Absence makes the heart grown fonder." With heifers, absence seems to make them forget because the heifer acted like she had no idea whose baby this was that we were shoving in front of her nose.

We decided to put them in the barn where they could be confined and get reacquainted. We got the heifer in a stall next to the other heifer with her swamp thing and went back to get the calf.

Getting the heifer to the barn, which is down a hill from our house and the pasture where we calve out the heifers, was not too difficult. Getting the calf that was too weak to walk very far was another matter.

The calf was too big to carry that far and had just enough fight in him that he wouldn't cooperate. As we mulled over our options I spied the kid's snow sled that we had sitting in the yard.

I'm not sure if it was a good idea or if we were just so tired it made sense, but we put the calf on the sled and launched him down the hill toward the barn. The idea was that we would run along side the sled and make sure he didn't fall off, but the sled was some kind of purple racer rocket and it went faster than we could keep up in the deep snow. All we could do was watch as the calf zoomed down the hill with his ears blown back and his nose in the air.

Miraculously the calf leaned from side to side with the dips and turns of the sled and managed to stay on. He reached the bottom of the hill, got off the sled and shook his head, slightly dazed from the adventure. The ride seemed to have invigorated him though and this time when we put him with his mother, the heifer didn't have the option of acting like she didn't know him. After a ride like that I guess he figured he was entitled to the "Breakfast of Champions."

If a Rancher Were President

There were a lot of good candidates vying for a chance to fill the presidential seat for the next four years, but I didn't see a single rancher in the bunch. Not even a movie actor who had a starring role in a western.

I'm guessing that most ranchers feel they don't have enough experience to be president, especially when it comes to foreign relations. But shoot just about every relationship ranchers have is somewhat foreign. Their cattle originated in Scotland, pigs from Asia, horses from Spain and their Honda from Japan. Their wives always come from out of town; otherwise, they would have known better.

Maybe the reason ranchers don't run for president is because they don't know which political party to sign up with. We've got the Democratic, Republican, Libertarian, Constitution and Green Parties. Ranchers could be affiliated with the Knee Deep In S**t Party, which is basically the same concept as a lot of the other parties anyway, just more descriptive.

Or how about the Poopulist Party? Ranchers are inherently members of this party anyway so it wouldn't be much of a stretch. The Grass Party sounds fitting, but I think that term was a bit overused in the 70s and meant something entirely different. The Mad Cow Party would be indicative of our times, but it probably wouldn't do much for the foreign export market. The Cow Rights Administration Party has a nice ring to it, but we have to be mindful of acronyms when selecting a name or we might end up with newspaper headlines like "Ranchers Nominate CRAP Leader", "CRAP Campaign Begins", "CRAP Creates Jobs", and "Stimulus Package Supported by CRAP."

Whatever we decide to call it, the main thing is to get ranchers on the ballot. They have a lot of skills that would help them in the role of president. For instance, ranchers are born leaders. If they can convince their wives to open and close gates in the middle of a snow blizzard while they sit in the warm truck cab, just think of the kind of power they would have over the senate.

Ranchers are also extremely organized in the midst of chaos. If a rancher were president, the Oval Office might get a little messy, but in that towering stack of papers, pocket knives and dead hot shot batteries on his desk, a rancher would still be able to find that all important cease fire order, eventually.

Ranchers are big on equal rights. They believe everyone should have an opportunity to help brand calves regardless of age, sex, race or time of day.

Ranchers are very resourceful and have learned to make do with whatever is on hand. For instance if a visiting dignitary such as Mikhail Gorbachev had a suspender or belt malfunction, a rancher president would have the necessary tools on hand — duct tape and bailing twine — to help him keep his pants up and prevent an embarrassing situation.

If a rancher were president, we wouldn't have to worry about another big Watergate scandal. A rancher would discretely open the Watergate at night when no one was watching.

Even if a rancher were voted in as vice president, he darn sure wouldn't mistake an attorney for a quail. If a rancher shot at an attorney — it wouldn't be an accident.

And I've never heard of a rancher doing anything questionable with a cigar, except maybe the time our neighbor Billy Bob McKrackin tried to get his pig to smoke one. But like another well-known politician, when asked if he is engaging in pig puffing Billy Bob said, "It depends on what the meaning of the word 'is' is. If 'is' means is and never has been, that is not— that is one thing. If it means there is none, that was a completely true statement."

"*The difference between 'involvement' and 'commitment' is like an eggs-and-ham breakfast: the chicken was 'involved' — the pig was 'committed'.*"
                    —*Unknown*

Grandma Got Run Over
by a Cow

Christmas always brings fond memories of family, friends, food, music, and of course cows. After all, for a rancher, what would Christmas be without cows? Those fond memories wouldn't be near as funny. The things we remember most from Christmases past are not the excitement of seeing a loved one open a present that was "just what they wanted" or the joy of singing carols or even the smell of the turkey basting in the oven.

No, what we remember are the Christmases that the turkey burned because the cows escaped and we had to chase them half the day to get them back in. Or how about the time the cows tipped one of their own upside down in the ditch and we had to spend Christmas morning pulling it out of a mud hole. The cows also broke through the yard gate and peered through the windows at us one year as we sat down to eat — thank goodness we were eating turkey!

That's why I don't understand why there aren't more Christmas songs about cows. No doubt you've heard the catchy little Christmas tune, "Grandma Got Run Over by a Reindeer." I think it is much more probable that Grandma would get run over by a cow than a fictitious flying reindeer for goodness sake. So I have taken it upon myself to rewrite the song as it probably really happened:

Grandma got run over by a cow,

walking to the barn on Christmas Eve.

You can say there's no such thing as mad cows

but as for me and other ranchers we believe.

She hadn't been drinking any eggnog,

and she hadn't eaten any fermented chow.

But she had forgotten to take her hotshot,

when she encountered that mad cow.

When we found her Christmas morning,

at the scene of the cow attack,

she had hoof-prints on her forehead,

and incriminating poop stains on her back.

Now we're all so proud of grandma,

she's been ranching for quite some time.

She rose up on her shaky feet,

and dusted off the snow and grime.

Grabbing whips and cussing like a truck driver,

she started swatting the cows from underneath.
It's not Christmas without Grandma,
chasing cows and looking for her teeth.

All the family's dressed in Carhartts (overalls),
watching Grandma put on quite a show.
The cows aren't going where she wants them
as she pursues them through the snow.

We just can't help but wonder,
should we save the cows and bring her back?
This is better than football
so we'll just leave her where she's at.

Now the prime rib is on the table,
and the wine is in the box.
Grandma came in to join us,
wearing clothes that smell like grandpa's socks.

I've warned all my friends and neighbors
better watch out for yourselves,
they should never let their grandma
go to the barn all by herself.

Grandma got run over by a cow,
walking to the barn on Christmas Eve.
You can say there's no such thing as mad cows
but as for me and other ranchers we believe.

Disclaimer: Any resemblance to grandmothers in our family to the one in this song is purely coincidental because I made all of this up.

I wish everyone a Christmas where blessings abound and those warm and fuzzy feelings come from the real reason for Christmas, not the cows nosing you in the armpits.

Mysteries and Makeup — the Tease Is On

When I was in grade school Tommy Bedwetter found out one day that I didn't like worms. Consequently, at every available opportunity, he would chase me around the school grounds at recess dangling a worm in my face.

Then there was Timmy Stinkington. Timmy found out that I didn't like having my hair pulled so every time I wore pigtails, which was pretty often in my early formative years, he would come up behind me and grab a braid in each of his grubby little hands and pull on them one at a time while bellowing as only a second grader can, "milk the cow, milk the cow."

Jimmy Dorksey also brings up taunting memories. Every time Dorksey walked by my desk, which seemed like every five minutes, he would use my face as a makeshift towel for his always-sticky hands while making a high pitched woo-woo-woo-woo sound similar to the Three Stooges.

Oddly enough, my teachers said the boys teased me because they knew I didn't like it, and to get my attention because they liked me. The teachers said if I would ignore them, they would stop it. Well, I tried ignoring them and they didn't "stop it" so gradually I handled the situations my own way.

One day when Stinkington came up behind me at recess and grabbed my hair I whirled around and grabbed a fist full of his short messy mane and pulled until he squealed like a girl. He was so surprised and embarrassed that he never pulled my hair again.

Likewise, the next time Dorksey wiped his hands across my face I bit his finger. That kind of backfired on me though. I didn't get in trouble. The teacher said he deserved it, but he screamed and cried and put up such a fuss that I felt so bad I started crying and the teacher had to call my mom to come and get me. But from then on Jimmy Dorksey walked wide circles around my desk.

The problem with the worm boy, though, kind of took care of itself. One day my Dad tired of baiting my hook for me when we went fishing and spent about three hours patiently teaching me to put the squirmy, slimy vermin on my own hook. After that, the next time Bedwetter shoved a worm in my face, no longer creeped out by them, I grabbed the worm and exclaimed, "Oh, isn't it cute!" I guess that kind of took the fun out of it because Bedwetter gave up the daily worm assaults.

The little boys eventually progressed to teenage boys, who knocked books out of my hands in the school hallways, and duct taped my locker shut, but I always held on to the belief that when they grew up and became men, they would stop this nonsense. Boy was I wrong!

Even after almost 20 years of marriage, if my husband discovers that there is something I don't like — that's exactly what he does. Over the years I have had to tolerate his high pitched whistling in my ear, his walking behind me giving me a shoe flat in the grocery store, and his chasing me around the ranch with a cattle hot shot.

I've tried to combat these things to no avail. When he whistles I sing in the loudest off key, tone deaf, voice I can muster, which seems to come natural for me anyway. But he can whistle louder and higher pitched than I can sing and always wins out.

I have tried stepping on the heels of his shoes in the grocery store, but it's hard to give someone a flat when he always wears boots. And as for the hot shot, well, I have to admit I'm no match for him and his swashbuckling prowess.

These things wouldn't be so bad, but unfortunately he keeps making new discoveries of things that I don't like. Lately, he has been reading gruesome serial murder mysteries before bedtime and tries to recount the details to me at breakfast. I keep telling him I don't like reading or hearing about Ivan the Impaler and Bob the Beheader and I wish he would keep it to himself.

"Oh," he says, faking an offended look, "I thought you would like to hear about it."

So I thought I would be adult and figure out a way to combat this without pulling his hair or biting his finger. After having to listen to his recent recount of his latest book and what Count Dracula did to his victims, in minuscule detail of course, I smiled and said, "That's nice. Oh, hey, did I tell you that I found this new shade of makeup that I think will match my complexion perfectly? It comes in about 25 different shades so it took me almost an hour to try out all the samples in the store, but it also has an SPF of 45. How lucky is that?"

He looked at me rather puzzled, but didn't say anything so I went on. "Oh, and I found this color of eye shadow that's to die for. It's blue, but not the harsh dark blue that you usually see. It's more of a light azure or sky blue with the faintest hint of shimmer to make my eyes really sparkle. And the store got in some new bronzing powder that I can hardly wait to try out, it's supposed to give you that sun kissed look…"

"Why in the heck are you telling me about this crap?" he finally interrupted.

"Oh," I smiled sympathetically, "I thought you would want to hear about it."

Seeing through my clever plan to make him listen to something that he doesn't care to hear about, too, he quickly recovered and said, "Oh, yes, I do want to hear about it because unlike you, if it's something that interests you, then it interests me. Tell me more."

So far neither one of us is budging, and our morning conversations center around the best type of makeup for combination skin, and what kind of knife Jack the Ripper used.

He says, "Did you know Jack used a four-inch blade on his victims as he…."

I interrupt, "I think in the pictures I've seen of Jack, he looks kind of pale, you know he could really benefit from just a touch of blush high on his cheek bones…Cover Girl has a new blush that has three different shades in one. Do you think Jack would look better in Purely Plum or Peach Perfection?"

I suppose we will eventually tire of this and move on when he discovers something else I don't like, but in the mean time I'm comforted by the thought that with all this teasing going on, we must really like each other a lot!

When Cows Sue

Almost every day when I watch the news or pick up the newspaper I see where people have sued someone. Lawsuits have been filed for everything from people suing restaurants for making them fat to suing the TV weatherman for predicting a sunny day that turned out to be rainy.

In one case a lawyer purchased a box of expensive and rare cigars, smoked each one of them, and then filed an insurance claim stating that the cigars were lost in a series of small fires. The insurance company refused to pay so the lawyer sued and won. The insurance company had to pay the lawyer $15,000 in the lawsuit, but the lawyer's victory was short lived. As soon as he cashed the check the insurance company had him arrested, charging him with 24 counts of arson.

All of this got me to thinking, if people could sue for things like this and in some cases actually win, I wonder what cows could sue for — tripping over a frozen cow patty while they were running across the field in the winter?

I got to asking around and discovered that our neighbor, Billy Bob McKrackin, was sued by his cows not too long ago. At first Billy Bob thought it was just a lot of bull, but it turns out the bulls had nothing to do with it. The cows obtained the services of an attorney, Iwanna Sueyou, who filed a class action lawsuit on their behalf alleging that Billy Bob refused to wear suspenders when he was feeding them.

Apparently without his suspenders, every time Billy Bob bends over to cut a bale of hay he gives the cows a clear view of...shall we say his version of the moon in broad daylight. In his defense, Billy Bob was a plumber before he became a rancher and didn't realize cows could be so offended by this.

In their suit, the cows claimed that seeing this side of Billy Bob threw them off their feed every day and caused a great deal of emotional trauma and physical discomfort. They cited loss of weight, lack of sleep due to visions of Billy Bob's backside dancing in their heads, and inability to chew their cud for several hours after seeing him, resulting in poor digestion and an excess of flatulence. This excess flatulence they contended is giving them unwanted attention from environmentalists who are blaming them for contributing to global warming.

"We have enough problems with bull trout and endangered weeds," Bossy, one of Billy Bob's cows stated to the Judge when their case went to court. "We don't need the added stress of being blamed for the loss of polar bear habitat as well."

Another cow was called to the stand. "We're so upset by Mr. McKrackin's backside, we can't produce milk half the time," Daisy bellowed as she sobbed into her hooves hoping to gain the Judge's sympathy.

Billy Bob representing himself, objected that the cows always had flatulence, only produced milk when they were fresh anyway, which is about half of the time, and to top it off they didn't wear suspenders either. The Judge allowed his case for flatulence and milk, but overruled his objection to suspenders saying that in their case tails were adequate.

The Judge, however, was learning in Billy Bob's favor until Sueyou made a bold, but shrewd move. Just as Billy Bob was stepping down from the witness stand, Sueyou dropped her notebook. When Billy Bob, being the polite man that he is, bent over to pick it up for her, he unintentionally, but adequately, demonstrated for the judge what the cows had been complaining about. Perry Mason couldn't have done a better job of exposing him.

With that Sueyou addressed the Judge saying, "No further witnesses, your honor. We rest our case."

The Judge said in all of his years in the courtroom he had never had a case where all at once the correct verdict was brought into view so clearly. He rapped his gavel on the bench and announced, "This Court finds in favor of the cows!" He then promptly excused himself from the Bench, asking the court clerk to find his Rolaids.

Billy Bob, now by order of the Court, wears both suspenders and a belt — at the same time.

This wasn't the first time though that Billy Bob had been sued by his livestock. Years ago one young cow sued him for a branding mishap. When Billy Bob applied his Triple X brand to her he slipped with the hot iron and it ended up looking like XXL. The cow claimed this mistake made her feel uncomfortable about her size and she sued him for emotional distress from poor self-esteem and missed breeding opportunities.

Like the insurance company with the cigars though Billy Bob got even. When the cattle market took a dive, he turned around and sued his cows for loss of wages and mental anguish.

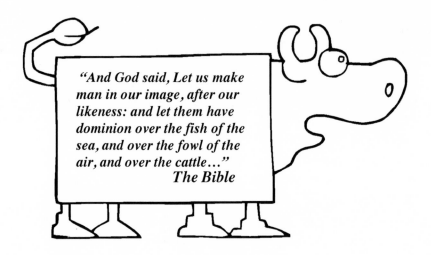

"*And God said, Let us make man in our image, after our likeness: and let them have dominion over the fish of the sea, and over the fowl of the air, and over the cattle...*"
                    The Bible

Computersanonymous.com

Time for a Computer Intervention

Our electricity went out a few days ago and the first thing I did was to go down to the basement to see if we threw a breaker switch. Naturally the basement is dark so I reached over to flip on the light switch to see where I was going. Apparently somewhere between my brain and my hand a vital piece of communication was lost – the electricity is out, therefore the lights don't work – duh!

Turns out it wasn't the breaker anyway, but I did have several other great duh moments that day. Pushing buttons, flipping switches and turning knobs likewise produced the same results – absolutely nothing.

I quickly came to two conclusions – that there is nothing to do when the electricity is out and I'm way too dependent on electric devices. I couldn't go more than 10 minutes without trying to turn something on or plug something in.

Of course there was no computer, no TV, I couldn't bake, no computer, no hot water, no cordless phone, no computer...wait...I'm starting to see a pattern here... After the 10th time in two hours of trying to turn my computer on, I cried out to my husband, "I think I'm addicted to my computer!"

"I told you that a long time ago," he said as he peered over the book he was reading.

"Yeah, but you're hardly ever right so I didn't bother to listen," I quipped back. "Besides, don't we have a generator somewhere? Maybe I could take the battery out of my car and rig up something to power my computer. Or maybe we could get the TV going – I wanted to play one of my exercise videos today."

"I don't think so," he said.

"But how am I ever going to get buns of steel?" I asked.

"Strap a bumper to your caboose perhaps," he muttered.

"What?" I said.

"Never mind, I think it's time for an intervention," he said as he plopped a rectangular shaped object in my lap.

"What's this?" I asked

"It's a book," he said.

"I know that," I said. "But what am I supposed to do with it?"

"You might try reading it," he offered.

"What a 'novel' idea!" I exclaimed. "Get it - 'novel'?"

"Yeah, I get it," he rolled his eyes.

I turned the book over in my hands examining the cover.

"There's no place to plug it in," he said watching me. "You just open it up like this," he said as he demonstrated with his book.

The urge to say "duh" was strong, but I managed to control myself.

"I need to get a lap top computer for emergencies like this because they run on batteries," I said

"A book sits on top of your lap; it is a lap top," he said.

"O.K. Mr. Smarty Pants," I said, "if it's a lap top, then how do you navigate without a mouse?"

"You don't need a mouse to navigate – it's called turning the pages."

"Oh, and here," he said as he ripped off the corner of the Sunday *Oregonian's* front page, "this is the save feature – you stick it between the pages so you can automatically go to that spot next time without having to search all over your hard drive."

"And this is a big one," he said, "a book never freezes or crashes."

"No," I said, "but it can go sailing through the air and accidentally wop you upside the head."

"Besides, you can't really compare a book to a computer," I said. "Where's the software, what applications do you use?"

"You use your imagination — you apply your brain," he said.

Seeing I wasn't going to get anywhere, I finally conceded. "O.K., I'll read a book," I said, "but not this book.

"What's wrong with that book – it's a good book," he said.

"'The Proper Care and Feeding of Husbands,'" by Dr. Laura," I said. "I don't think so. I don't have enough imagination available on my internal hard drive for that and I think my brain would completely freeze causing me to crash on the couch or at the very least go into sleep mode."

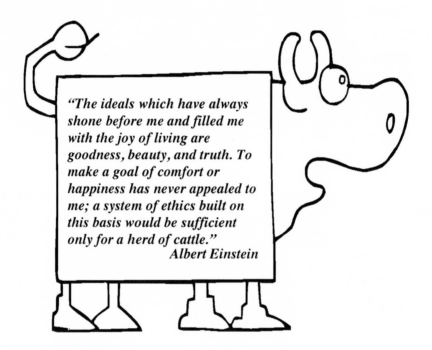

"The ideals which have always shone before me and filled me with the joy of living are goodness, beauty, and truth. To make a goal of comfort or happiness has never appealed to me; a system of ethics built on this basis would be sufficient only for a herd of cattle."
Albert Einstein

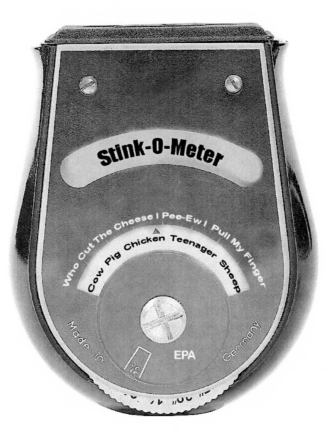

Toot Tax

It has come to my attention that there is an evil plot in the works — so deadly, so disruptive — that it could be the end of civilization as we know it. The Environmental Protection Agency (EPA) wants to charge ranchers for the gas emitted by their cows through belching and flatulence. It would require those with more than 50 beef cattle to pay an annual fee of $87.50 per head.

They came up with these figures by scientifically testing cows with a "Stink-o-meter." The Stink-o-meter measures cow flatulence ranging from "I didn't do it" and "Who cut the cheese" to "Did something die?" They averaged the results and came up with $0.02 per head. Then they added in $87.48 per head as part of a rancher-funded economic stimulus package to give to financial institutions and car manufacturers in dire need of corporate jets to take CEOs on vacation.

Of course, we ranchers don't mind paying exorbitant and unfair fees, but it would be nice to see a few tax deductions to help offset our toot tax. For instance, if we could claim our cows as dependents, after all they do live with us 12 months out of the year and we are their sole providers, that would go a long ways toward compensating us for our losses.

The biggest problem I see with this toot tax is that cows aren't the only stinkers. Of course they already figured out hogs would need to be taxed, about $20 per head. That was a no brainer because even with a heavy duty Stink-o-meter that tests up to "Did something die, get buried and then dug up three weeks later?" it was off the scale with hogs. In fact in one instance, on a 500 head hog farm, the Stink-o-meter simply exploded.

But I don't think they have checked out chickens yet. Although they are small, the phrase, "What smells like rotten eggs?" originated from someone who was familiar with fowl flatulence.

Sheep on the other hand release enough gas into the air to fuel a truck for 25 miles. You can't blame the EPA though for not knowing that, as sheep are pretty good at pulling the wool over your eyes.

Horses can toot with the best of them and are about the loudest of them all, preferring to let their methane into the air with a lot of fanfare. They don't try to conceal it and are usually quite proud of their accomplishments so it would be easy to get the old Stink-o-meter reading on them.

Wiener dogs are also quite gaseous for their size. While they are seemingly engrossed in trying to give your face a good washing, they will expel gas out the other end without making a sound. Thus the term "silent, but deadly."

And let's not forget the free-range stinkers like deer and elk. It would be rather difficult to get the Stink-o-meter close enough to measure their gas, but rest assured, since they eat the same diet as cattle, usually out of the same haystack, they would register pretty high on the Sink-o-meter somewhere in the vicinity of "No, they don't smell like wildflowers" and "Pee-ew."

Probably the guiltiest of the methane gas emitters, though, are American teenagers. If the EPA could tax these trouser rippers, there would be no reason to tax livestock. The cost per head could be figured out by their individual diets with the most expensive taxes being placed on those who eat fast food hamburgers more than three times per week where the beef was imported from Brazil and other countries. The restaurants could also be charged a fee for contributing to the emissions of minors.

I think the best way to determine who the biggest stinkers are would be to place the Stink-o-meter near those responsible for making laws in the EPA. I bet it would read, "Pull my finger" pretty consistently.

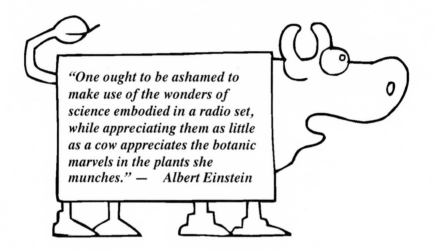

"*One ought to be ashamed to make use of the wonders of science embodied in a radio set, while appreciating them as little as a cow appreciates the botanic marvels in the plants she munches.*" — *Albert Einstein*

Defending the Grass

It was a dark and stormy night. I had just slipped off into a deep slumber — a deep, snoreless slumber (contrary to what my husband says, I don't snore) — when two shots rang out piercing the silence.

I bolted upright in bed. I sat and listened. Other than a coyote howling in the distant hills, the night was silent. That is if you don't count the gentle hum of the computer downstairs, the constant revving of the refrigerator, and the bulls bellowing in the pasture. And, oh yeah, a dark and stormy night tends to make a little racket too.

But, still, everything seemed normal, so I lay back down and just as I dozed off again — kaboom, kaboom!

This time I knew it wasn't my snoring…er, ah, I mean the storm, so I reached over and flipped on the bedside lamp. I immediately noticed that my husband had pushed all of the blankets over to my side of the bed. He does that pretty often although he has a funny name for his generosity. He calls me a "bed hog." Oh, and a few minutes later I also noticed that he wasn't in the bed. I'm pretty observant that way.

I cautiously peered over the edge of the bed to see if I had accidentally kicked him onto the floor in my sleep. Usually I just fake being asleep when I do that, but there's always a first time for everything.

Before I could get my head back up from over the edge of the bed, I heard it again — kaboom, kaboom. Now that I was wide-awake, it was so loud it startled me and I whacked my head on the edge of the nightstand.

This time I could tell the noise was coming from outside. I crawled out of bed and looked out the window. I gasped at what I saw. It was truly a sight that dark and stormy nights are known for. There in the moonlight stood a man in a trench coat and rubber boots holding a rifle!

"Oh my gosh," I thought. "There's a dangerous criminal, probably a pervert or Lord only knows what else, lurking right outside our bedroom window and my husband and supposedly protector is nowhere around."

As my eyes struggled to focus into the darkness the shape standing in the field began to look vaguely familiar. It wasn't a trench coat, it was a bathrobe, and the boots were of the irrigating variety. O.K. the mystery of my husband's disappearance was solved – he was the dangerous criminal/pervert standing in the field.

But what in the heck was he doing? He pointed the shotgun into the air and fired, kaboom, kaboom.

"Egad," I thought, "he's trap shooting using the stars as targets instead of clay pigeons!"

I threw open the window. "I know you need all the practice you can get," I yelled, "but for crying out loud, can't you shoot at the stars some other time — some other time…oh I don't know… besides midnight!"

Kaboom, Kaboom!

Having received such a rude response, I slammed the window shut and went back to bed.

A few minutes later he walked into the bedroom.

"For your information, I wasn't shooting at the stars, I was trying to scare the elk away before they eat all of the cow pasture," he said rather irritated.

"Oh, sorry," I said. "Usually you do that in your underwear with pots and pans. The rubber boots and the trench coat threw me."

"Trench coat?" he asked.

"Never mind," I said.

We're going on our fifth night now of shooing somewhere around 100 head of elk out of the pasture.

I say "we" even though I'm not actually the one running around in the middle of the night with a shotgun, because I'm suffering the sleep deprivation side effects from it. The elk hazing doesn't happen at the same time every night, but it's always "after" I get to sleep.

My husband can be sound asleep on the couch with the TV blaring, while the neighbors are visiting with him, and when the dog is hocking up something dead in the middle of the living room floor, but one little far off squeal of a cow elk and he jolts awake faster than a teenager on Red Bull (an energy drink). It doesn't even have to be a full squeal. It can be an elk hiccup a mile away and he's armed and ready to defend his grass!

He started out by sneaking up on the elk, while they were all standing by the fence peering into the pasture watching him. Pretty soon though they got to where they were coming in closer every night and weren't far enough away to sneak up on. So he began defending the area from our yard. It's a good thing we don't have wagons or I'm sure we would have to circle them every night before going to bed.

And even though I know it's going to happen sometime in the middle of the night, and he says I should be used to it by now, every time it does, for some reason, unbeknownst to my husband, I just can't seem to sleep through the sound of a double barrel shotgun going off right outside the bedroom window.

I told my husband at breakfast this morning that I'm going to check into a sleep center.

"That's a good idea," he said. "Maybe they can do something about your snoring."

"No, I mean so I can get some sleep," I said. "And for the last time, I don't snore!"

"What do you think wakes me up every night?" he said. "I use your snoring as an alarm to get up to listen for the elk. It works pretty good during calving season too."

I'm thinking I just might have one of those episodes tonight where I "accidentally" kick him over the edge of the bed while I'm asleep...and I think he's going to be very generous with the blankets!

The Feng Shui Ranch

I recently read a book on Feng Shui and how to "create your sacred space." Feng Shui is the ancient Chinese practice of the placement and arrangement of space, including things that take up space, to achieve harmony with the environment. Apparently when your space is properly positioned, you will be receptive to good fortune.

It was quite interesting and it got me to wondering how Feng Shui principles could be applied on the ranch. So I told my husband that we needed to assess "our space" and see if we were in balance.

"We probably should," he said, "but I don't want to."

Since the burden of determining if we are in balance was left up to me, I started with what I thought was a logical area, the barn. The book says that the area surrounding the entrance should be completely clear. So I picked up a couple of buckets sitting outside near the barn door that we use to grain the young bulls. Keeping in mind that the book says, if you have to have clutter keep it off the ground, I hung them on a nail inside a stall in the barn.

Next, there was a stack of salt block trays that I neatly placed inside the stall out of sight along with a few livestock whips.

This stall was quickly becoming what the book described as a "junk room." Junk rooms, the book says, will have a negative impact on some area of your life. Since I couldn't figure out what area of my life was being negatively affected by a junk stall, I decided it was O.K. to have one and proceeded to put several more things in it. After all that clutter has to go somewhere if we are going to achieve my goal of having a Feng Shui Ranch.

Inside the barn, various items such as halters, hotshots, ropes, covered barrels full of cat food, grain and oats, syringes and medicines lined the walls and floor. Wow, this barn is just full of clutter I thought to myself. No wonder our flow of energy is restricted. It's not that we are getting older after all; our Feng is just out of sync with our Shui. So I gathered up everything that wasn't nailed down and shoved it into the junk stall.

I briefly wondered if clutter also included dried up cow poop, but quickly decided that since it's organic material, it could be considered part of the ground, rather than something on the ground, and could remain where it was.

Satisfied that I had achieved the proper balance in the barn, I went outside and looked around at other areas that might need to be cleared of negative energy.

I spotted a cow that was standing in the corrals and wondered if she would benefit from space clearing. The book says moving a person's energy can help clear out negative feelings. Since this cow had been kind of ornery when we gave her a shot the day before, I thought it might be worth a try.

As I approached her, I tried to sense her electromagnetic energy by waving my hands gently through the air. When I thought I felt a little tingling sensation, I tried to engage her energy so I could move out her negative vibes and replace them with positive ones. I wasn't sure which direction to move the energy so I tried moving it to the left and the right. As it turns out that tingling sensation I felt, I suspect is similar to the one that people get just before lightning strikes them. The cow did not respond well to having her energy moved, so she used all of that negative energy she had bottled up to run me out of the corral.

I was somewhat confused because I had read that in some countries, the cow is considered to be a sacred animal that represents good fortune. (I'm suspecting that this is probably where the term "holy cow" originated.) In fact, a cow seated on a pile of gold ingots is believed to be a very potent Feng Shui symbol. But since we don't happen to have a pile of gold lying around, and I doubt that we could get a cow to sit on it anyway, I will just have to take the writer's word for it.

After that encounter, I decided that cows must have their own way of attaining Feng Shui. If you get in their space, they will clear you out! So I decided to leave the cows alone for now and go back to the house and move some energy and dust around with the vacuum cleaner. A few hours later, my husband came dragging himself into the house just exhausted.

"What's wrong?" I asked.

"Well, I got a cow out of the back pasture and managed to get her all the way up to the barn to give her a shot for foot rot and couldn't find the medicine or syringes," he said as he collapsed on the couch. "I had her in the chute, but couldn't make her go forward into the head catch because I couldn't find the hotshot. Then the bulls in the pen next to us got excited and started running around getting her upset so I thought I would toss them a little grain to quiet them down, while I looked for the medicine. But I couldn't find the buckets or the grain. The cats were pawing all over me in the barn wanting to be fed, but I couldn't even find the dang cat food."

"Then, to make matters worse," he continued, "that cow we got in yesterday to give a shot charged me when I went into the corral. I don't know what the heck her problem is. She's never done that before."

"Oh, my gosh!" I said, trying to sympathize with his plight and nonchalantly sneak out of the room.

"Wait a minute," he said, now on his feet with his hands on hips looking directly at me. "You wouldn't happen to know anything about all of this, would you?"

Sensing that this would not be a good time to try to move his energy, I told him about my efforts to achieve harmony and balance on the ranch.

Needless to say I am banned from trying to move a cow's energy in any direction, and now I know why a junk stall/room can have a negative impact on my energy. By the time I got everything moved back to where it was supposed to be, I was pooped!

I Don't Know...

I thought when I was a child that some day I would know, but now it doesn't appear that I will ever know.

I can remember as far back as the age of 5 when there was so much that I didn't know that I didn't know I didn't know it. Even so my parents kept asking me anyway.

"Who left the door open?"

"I don't know."

"Whose turn is it to set the table?"

"I don't know."

"Who spilled grape juice on the sofa?"

"I don't know."

You would think that as the years progressed that they would finally realize that I didn't know, but they never stopped trying to find out if there was indeed something that I might know.

In my teenage years the questions changed somewhat, but my response was always the same.

"How did that dent get in my car?"

"I don't know."

"Why are you so late getting home?"

"I don't know."

"How many times have I told you not to wear that?"

"I don't know." (In my defense, this was a trick question because I didn't know I was supposed to be keeping track.)

Of course there were times that I made an effort to provide different, somewhat revealing answers, but it never lasted very long as they would inevitably get around to asking me something I didn't know.

"Where are you going tonight?"

"Just around."

"Whom are you going with?"

"The gang."

"What are you going to do?"

"Nothin'."

"How long are you going to do nothin'?"

"I don't know."

It was tough going through life not knowing so when I became an adult I studied hard, took college classes and learned many things. As it turns out though, most of the time the things I learned were things that no one else wanted to know.

Then when I was blessed with a child, I thought finally, someone who knows less than I do that I can teach what little I know to. Turns out this not knowing stuff must be hereditary because whenever I asked him a question like my parents asked me, he didn't know either.

Eventually though after marrying a rancher, I learned how to know… for the most part.

"Who left the corral gate open?"

"The cows must have pushed it open."

"Where's my shovel?"

"The dog must have taken it."

"Who's been riding my four-wheeler?"

"Here, have a doughnut."

Now that I'm older and wiser though it's much easier because I conveniently forget what I don't know…

"*The mere brute pleasure of reading — the sort of pleasure a cow must have in grazing.*"

Lord
Chesterfield

Missed It by that Much!

Puddin' Head, our black lab Lord only knows what cross dog pretty much has the run of the ranch. She diligently protects the place from intruders of the four-legged variety, but she's not the bravest when it comes to critters that are larger than her.

The cows are especially worrisome to Puddin' because although she doesn't think they have any business coming close to the house, they have chased her on occasion, which is a scenario she's not too eager to repeat. So in order to avoid having to run back to the safety of the porch and keep her dignity intact, she chases cows away from the house under the gate and fence. She steps back toward the middle of the yard, gets her hackles up and her teeth out, and runs snarling and barking full speed toward the fence and the offending cow. Once she gets to the fence, she puts on the brakes, and ducks her head under the fence just enough to give the cow a good look at her fierce attack and then makes a hasty retreat.

The cow in turn is startled by the sudden noise and movement, jumps sideways and then trots off into the field with her head and tail held high trying to regain her composure.

This system works pretty well for Puddin' most of the time, except in the early spring when the ground is wet and muddy like it is now. She will go through the same motions, get a run at it, duck her head and slam on the brakes. Only this time of year when she puts on the brakes she keeps sliding forward in the slick mud and finds herself back peddling on the other side of the fence trying to stop. By then she has become precariously close to the cow, which scares her and she starts yelping. While the cows are usually startled by a fiercely snarling and running dog; a yelping, sliding, slightly embarrassed dog seems to make them mad and they quickly chase her back under the fence with her muddy tail between her legs.

This type of commotion goes on every morning with the cows and Puddin' Head so we've gotten used to it and for the most part don't pay much attention to it any more. Last week, however, as she was going through her usual paces, I heard a strange yipping sound unlike her cow chasing, can't stop in time yelping, and when I looked out the window, I saw a coyote was hot on her heels and following her right up to the house.

I ran to the closet and grabbed the only gun I knew was loaded, a .22 rifle, and by the time I got outside Puddin' had made it safely to the back porch. The coyote stood about 20 yards away obviously trying to decide whether or not to risk coming in closer for a Puddin' snack. As soon as it saw me though, no doubt it had heard of my legendary marksmanship, the coyote turned tail and ran. It went about 150 yards out in the pasture and stopped, turning to look back at us. I think it was having second thoughts about the whole situation and was wondering if a woman in a robe and pink fuzzy slippers with a dog hiding behind her was a very big threat. But that's where it made its big mistake; it should have kept on running.

I raised the rifle, aimed right between its beady eyes and fired. The bullet whizzed out of the barrel with a piercing scream (well, as piercing as a .22 can get) and sailed through the air directly toward its intended target. There was a fleeting moment that I was feeling kind of sorry for the coyote at having had the misfortune of trying to kill the dog of a sharp shooter like myself. But before I had a chance to ponder it further, the bullet hit with a dull thud. The coyote, obviously stunned, looked down for a split second before shaking off the remnants of a half dried up cow pie I had hit next to him, and took off running with an amazing burst of speed.

Puddin' didn't care that I had missed the coyote, she was just satisfied that the coyote was running away from her instead of at her. She came out from behind me, did a little happy dance and yelled at the coyote in her canine language, which roughly translated into English as "Yeah, and don't come back either."

About that time my husband who unbeknownst to me was watching the whole thing from the barn yelled rather sarcastically, "Good shot, dear!"

"I wasn't trying to hit it," I yelled back in my defense, "I just wanted to scare it off. And as you can see it worked."

That remark I made, once he got back to the house, was immediately followed by a lecture. "If you are going to shoot at a coyote you need to try to hit it," he said. "Otherwise it will learn to run just out of range when it sees us and continue to try to get the dog when we're not looking."

After about another 10 minutes of him lecturing me, I couldn't take it any more. Like a thief being interrogated under a hot spotlight, I broke down. "All right, all right," I said. "I was trying to hit the blasted thing and I missed. But I only missed it by that much," I said as I held my fingers about two inches apart.

I'm sure he was astonished as he had never known me to miss before, but he hid his surprise well by laughing for the next two hours.

Later in the day, he asked me, "Why didn't you just tell me to start with that you missed?"

I immediately thought of all kinds of excuses, including the obvious fact that I don't like lectures, but finally said, "Well, Vice President Dick Cheney didn't have to say anything for 24 hours when he missed the quail and shot the lawyer last year. I figured I could get away with it for a little while."

Mutiny at the Sale Yard

We took our steers to the sale yard last week hoping to slip in, drop off our critters in two trips, and be home by lunch. But it didn't quite work that way; in fact, it didn't work like anything we had ever imagined.

The first load went smooth. We pulled up to the sale yard's unloading area, which consists of a system of gates that allows you to drive your stock trailer through, stop while the gate behind you is closed and then swing open the trailer door, which ideally closes off any gap at the side for livestock to slip through. The steers bounded out of the trailer and trotted down the alleyway into the sale yard like all good little steers should.

When we went back home to load the second group of steers we decided since it was a smaller load we should take a couple of older cows that we wanted to cull out of the herd along to the sale. While we were at it we threw in another cow that was younger, but had a bad attitude. We loaded four cows into the trailer and closed a panel separating them and the steers for the 30-minute trip to the sale yard.

Just like the first group of steers the second group unloaded without any problems and trotted down the alley. However, the cows, being cows, weren't quite as obliging. Oh, all four of them jumped out of the trailer and headed down the alley all right, but only two reached their intended destination. They had planned a mutiny.

I was still sitting in the pickup when all of the sudden I heard someone yell "shut the gate!" I looked out the side mirror just in time to see my husband, Mike, come flying over the fence with a cow's head expediting the process considerably by making contact with his backside.

Before I had a chance to jump out and see what was going on, the trailer, still attached to the pickup, began to shake violently. I leaned over and looked out the other side mirror to see a cow, oh, not just any cow, but our big fat cow, trying to wiggle her way through a two-foot gap between the trailer and the gate. Two men who worked at the sale yard ran out in front of her and began bopping her on the head with plastic ball-bearing-filled paddles to try and make her back up. Unfortunately, this just made her mad and when she finally freed her hips from the cumbersome livestock trailer that was attached to her rear end like a hula skirt, she was one ticked off bovine. She charged at the men, narrowly missing them, before running after another cow that being slightly thinner, had squirted out in front of her without me even seeing her.

The sale yard is next to a busy highway so naturally that is where the cows headed. Apparently, what little information I could get out of my husband as we sped after the cow dragging the livestock trailer in tow, was that the two cows for no visible reason about half way down the alley had decided to turn around and put the livestock sale yard as far behind them as possible, and as quickly as possible.

In the meantime, one of the sale yard guys had hopped on a four-wheeler and sped after them, but was bucked off when the machine flipped over on its back when it hit the pavement of the highway. Before we could jump out of the pickup to see if he was O.K., he gave us the thumbs up signal, up-righted the four-wheeler and continued his pursuit of our wayward cows.

The cows were actually headed for home, and I believe if they had known how to navigate the freeway exit ramp would have made it. They were temporarily sidetracked, though, by a nearby pasture. The lead cow kept going, but the other one jumped the fence into the pasture. However, she didn't follow the age old advice of "look before you leap" and landed smack dab in the middle of a muddy and full irrigation ditch and couldn't get up. By this time several sale yard cowboys were in hot pursuit. They roped her head and pulled giving her the extra oomph she needed to crawl to safety narrowly avoiding the need for mouth-to-mouth resuscitation. Although, the sale yard cowboys are a dedicated and hardworking bunch, it's probably fortuitous that she didn't need that.

As they worked at getting her into a livestock trailer, Mike and I pursued the lead cow that had also jumped into the pasture further down the road. As I wasn't close enough to see, I can only imagine the look on her face — something along the lines of "oh sh**!" — when she realized she had jumped into a portion of the pasture that contained five strapping young bulls. We found out quickly that selling her was a good move as it was obvious she hadn't gotten bred this summer — she was very much in heat and the bulls had picked up on that before her feet even hit the ground.

The sale yard cowboys once again came to the rescue, roping her on horseback. Getting her into our trailer with the bulls still clamoring for her attention was an event in itself. After several unsuccessful attempts, they finally threaded the rope through the trailer and while Mike pulled, they backed up another stock trailer, which gave her the incentive, in the way of a bump on the caboose, to get in the trailer.

On the way back to the sale yard, we stopped briefly to visit with a woman who had been helping with the runaway cow roundup. She made the comment that the cows were probably worth a little money to someone so it was lucky that they didn't have to be shot. We got a good laugh out of that until Mike mentioned that they were our cows. She didn't seem to be laughing quite so much after he shared that with her.

The other cow had already been taken back to the sale yard and while we were waiting in line to unload this one a seasoned cowboy ambled up to our pickup window and said with a look of sincerity concealed behind a sideways grin, "Looks like you had a stray."

As we were visiting, Mike mentioned that the cow still had a rope around her neck and she didn't seem too agreeable to him going in the trailer to take it off so hopefully they could get her in a chute to remove it.

"Don't worry," said the cowboy. "We've got some greenhorns here who can take care of that."

As it turns out, it was a good thing that the rope was still around her head because as soon as we unloaded her, it was like an instant replay. She whirled around and managed to squirm through a gap on the other side between the gate and trailer. This time it was a little easier from my perspective in the pickup to see what took place. In the side view mirror I saw several people high tail it over the fence just before her big black nose struck the mirror and folded it in.

Several of the men took off running after her, only for a little while it was hard to tell if she was chasing them or the other way around. It was like watching an old silent movie, the men would run by me chasing the cow and then a few minutes later the whole group would come tearing by again only with the cow chasing them.

Mike finally managed to get a hold of the rope and was soon aided by two other guys who grabbed the rope. The cow ran all around the livestock yard with the three men in tow hanging on to the rope until she finally went into a grassy area where they were able to run a couple of laps around a tree and stop her.

This time they backed the trailer clear into the alleyway and deposited her directly into a sorting pen. Since we were well past our noon deadline of having the fiasco over with, we decided to stay and watch the sale to see how much our steers would bring.

As we were sitting by the sale ring I noticed several women come in who were wearing pretty sequined jackets, freshly pleated Wranglers and shiny Ariat boots. I looked down at my faded cow pooped splattered jeans, my rubber boots caked with the same, and my old sweatshirt and said to Mike, "Obviously, they didn't have to help their husbands sort cattle this morning."

"No," he said as he patted my hand. "And they didn't get here early enough to watch the cow mutiny either. Just think of all they missed out on."

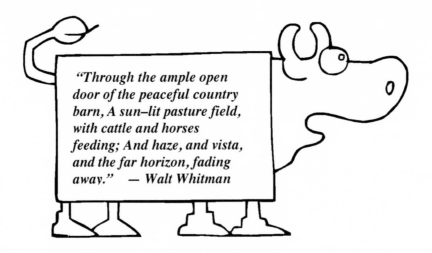

"Through the ample open door of the peaceful country barn, A sun–lit pasture field, with cattle and horses feeding; And haze, and vista, and the far horizon, fading away."   — Walt Whitman

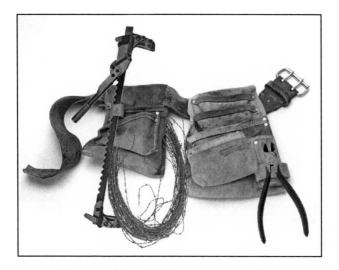

Tool Belts for Everyone!

I've been studying the different professions and have come to the conclusion that carpenters, electric linemen and police officers have a big advantage over ranchers. They all have some type of belt with compartments that hold their tools. Everything they need to complete a job, whether it's a screwdriver, needle nosed pliers or handcuffs, is within easy reach when they need it.

Almost everyone could use some kind of tool belt, with the exception of plumbers of course who don't need any extra weight dragging their britches down when they squat to look under the bathroom sink. But think of how handy a tool belt would be in the kitchen with compartments for salt and pepper, a spatula, spoons and even loops to hang frying pans and a couple of ham hocks on.

Lawyers instead of a briefcase could have the executive tool belt, which would surely hold all of our money and a small credit card scanner to save them countless trips to the bank.

Doctors could have medical tool belts with places for thermometers, tongue depressors, and rubber gloves as well as a variety of built in pill dispensers. They could also include a Cheez-it's dispenser just to be polite as in, "I'm sorry to tell you Mrs. McKrackin, your gallbladder will have to come out, but here, have a Cheeze-it."

Teachers could really use tool belts. If they could carry a supply of Kleenexes and cups of water, kids would rarely have to get out of their seats.

Politicians would have a much easier time if they had tool belts. Since they never seem to be able to "reach a consensus," they could carry their consensus in their tool belt within easy reach along with that box they are always trying to think outside of. Then, they could periodically reach into their tool belt and "revisit" them whenever they wanted to.

And think of how much cooler pencil pushers would look if they carried their writing utensils in a tool belt instead of pocket protectors. They would also have room for their PDAs, cell phones, pagers and spare tape for their eyeglasses without having to wear a fanny pack.

The uses for tool belts are virtually endless. That's why I don't understand when I mentioned to my husband how convenient a tool belt would be for ranchers that he didn't jump at the chance to try to make one. I really thought I was on to something — a rancher's tool belt could hold everything from calf scour medicine to a quick release hotshot. And the tool belt could even be fastened with a big shiny rodeo buckle.

"Just think of how handy a tool belt would be for repairing fences," I tried to convince him. "Instead of digging through a rusty coffee can full of greasy bolts and bent nails mixed with pieces of hay for a couple of fence staples, you could have a compartment right on your tool belt for them. Think of the time it would save you and the wear and tear on your fingers from jabbing them with sharp objects in the can."

"You wouldn't have to rummage around behind your pickup seat any more for wire stretchers because they would be securely strapped in your tool belt," I added.

"And what about the hammer?" I asked. "It's always hidden under a pile of papers and Hostess Ding Dong wrappers in your jockey box. Think of all the trips you could save from having to go back to the pickup every time you need the wire cutters or the crow bar."

"Well," he said, "my pickup is my tool belt and I don't have to dig through a can jabbing my fingers or search behind the seat or in the jockey box for my tools. That's why I bring you with me to fix fences. Sounds like you're the one who needs the tool belt, to pack all of my stuff. And while you're at it make sure you have a slot in your belt to hold my coffee."

Since that conversation, I've decided that what ranchers really need is a hard hat. It could be shaped like a cowboy hat and worn to protect them from falling bales of hay, close encounters with mad cows and the occasional flying frying pan, conveniently extracted from the kitchen tool belt of course.

There was an old man who said, "How Shall I flee from this horrible cow? I will sit on this stile, and continue to smile, which may soften the heart of that cow."

Edward Lear

Great Galloping Heifers!

I get a kick out of working baby calves through the chute. Seriously, I do, they kick me every chance they get. In spite of their lower limb jabs and hooks though, they aren't very big and can't do much damage to my shins. In fact I enjoy being around them so I always jump at the chance to help with the little buggers. That's why when my husband asked me to help him work the heifer calves a few weeks ago I didn't have any qualms about it whatsoever.

Being the nice guy that he is, my husband warned me that these calves were a little larger than the ones I was used to helping him with, and he graciously volunteered to call one of his friends to help if I didn't think I could handle it. Now, I don't know about other ranch wives, but asking me if I can handle it — them's fighting words. You better believe I can handle it! And on the outside chance that I can't, I will never admit it!

So fortified with too much pride and several peanut butter cookies I marched out to the corrals this cold November day with my Carhartt overalls on and my hackles up. As we began herding the 8-month-old heifers from the feed bunk into the corrals I immediately noticed something odd. For some reason when calves are out in the pasture running around, they look much smaller than when they are standing next to you. Good grief, I thought to myself, these critters are just a few short months and a half dozen head butts from becoming full-grown cows. And, as I soon discovered, they were each about 500 pounds of pure stubbornness, a trait passed on from their equally uncooperative mothers.

My job, the one I always volunteer for with the baby calves, was to run each heifer up the chute because although they were bigger, they were still small enough that they could turn around in the chute. My husband worked the head catch and a local veterinarian, Mark, bangs vaccinated the heifers because a legal record and identification number of it is required. I used to think that bangs vaccinations were what gave cows their stylish haircuts, but have since learned that it prevents a disease called brucellosis.

I was a little concerned about the size of these critters, but the first heifer ran right up the chute at a full gallop with hardly any prodding from me — that is until she came to the head catch. The minute her nose touched the opening she put on her brakes and skidded to a stop on the muddy ground. Since I was running behind her and didn't expect her to stop I almost rear-ended her. And believe me, rear-ending a heifer of any size is a very smelly proposition. She immediately turned around and forced her way past me. There really wasn't enough room for both of us to stand side by side so she squeezed me flat like an almost empty tube of toothpaste and stepped on my foot on her way by.

This was about the time it crossed my mind that I really wished people could be smashed flat and then pop up unscathed ready to run again like a cartoon character. But, since I didn't have that capability, and two men were waiting at the head catch for my next amazing feat, I hobbled down the chute after her mumbling the same words that made Bugs Bunny famous – "Of course, you realize, this means war!"

I maneuvered her down the chute again at a full gallop, and just like before she skidded to a stop before entering the head catch, only this time I was prepared and grabbed her head and pushed it forward before she could manage to turn around. After what seemed like hours, probably two minutes in reality, and much poking, prodding and pushing on my part she finally stepped into the head catch.

The next few used the same method — galloping up the chute, skidding to a stop and trying to turn around — but just as I was getting down a routine, a gargantuan heifer came through. She was used to throwing her weight around and not quite as timid as the others. Like the other heifers though she galloped up the chute and skidded to a stop, but rather than trying to turn around, she backed up. By then the muddy ground in the chute had turned into a combination of regular mud stuff mixed with heifer natural fertilizer stuff and was so slick I couldn't get any traction. Despite my best efforts of using my body as a human roadblock, she shoved me all the way back down the chute like a cross country skier with an 80-mile an hour tail wind.

I prodded her into the chute again, and as I was running behind her yelling, poking and flapping my arms, I slipped in the muddy slime and fell down. Fortunately my flailing around in the mud and crud like a wounded flamingo scared her enough that she kept going forward, but once again, she skidded to a stop right before entering the head catch.

I learned a long time ago that the closer you stand to a calf's back end, as unpleasant as that is, the harder it is for them to kick you. They can't get enough distance between you and their foot to really let you have it. And after I managed to stand up I had enough slime on my Carhartts to star in an alien invasion movie so trying to avoid her bovine derrière was no longer a problem. I got a run at it and plowed into her similar to a football guard clearing a path for the quarterback. I lambasted her with everything I had — and she didn't budge an inch.

As the veterinarian and my husband continued coaxing me "come on, push, push, push, you can do it" I began to wonder which one of them would finally announce, "congratulations — it's a healthy, bouncing baby girl!"

After what seemed like an eternity of my shouting and shoving, the veterinarian finally leaned over the chute and gave her a little tickle with his fingers on her back. This little tickle for some reason, after my plowing into her upwards of 50 miles an hour, and slapping, yelling, prodding and elbowing her, doing everything except putting on a big bad wolf Halloween mask, startled her and she jumped right into the head catch.

There were only 25 heifer calves to work that day, but to justify the stiffness and soreness I suffered for days afterward, let's say there were at least 100 calves that I had to shove up the chute. And while we're at it let's say I did this single-handedly through four feet of snow in the worst blizzard this area has ever had and the chute was situated on a 45-degree angle uphill, both ways. Oh, yeah — I can handle it!

Bottle Brats

Feeding one calf from a bottle is fun. Feeding more than one is like throwing yourself in a pond of piranhas and hoping you will make it out alive.

The calves will rush in and attack you from all sides trying to wrap their lips around everything from your shoelaces to your elbow. And when you tell them the milk is "all gone" they react similar to a 2-year-old child who has had his daily quota of sugar and wants more. All gone doesn't mean diddley squat to a screaming 2-year-old and likewise calves think you could surely come up with something if they just head butted you long enough and hard enough.

I fed two orphaned calves this year, "Tri" and "Tip." Tri was abused by his mother, a young heifer that kicked him every time he tried to have dinner, and Tip was a twin that was abandoned by her mother in favor of her larger brother. So you can see they both had "issues" coming into this new feeding relationship.

I helped them work through their anger and abandonment problems by providing them with knees, thighs and hips to head butt as well as toes to stomp on. After 10 minutes of messing me up good during feeding times, they always felt better about their situations.

They had a pretty good buddy system worked out similar to Demolition and the New Age Outlaws, WWE wrestling tag teams. While Tri would start rooting around at my behind, Tip would go for my armpit. It wouldn't matter that I had the bottles right in front of their faces, they would have to exhaust all other possibilities of where they thought milk might come from first. Once they were satisfied that milk was not forthcoming from my pant leg, they finally latched on to the bottles' rubber udders.

For a glorious five seconds, they were totally content, sucking and gulping the milk down into their rumbling stomachs. The wonderful feeling of a baby animal leaning against your legs bonding with you is only surpassed by the wonderful feeling of getting the heck out of their pen before they attack again.

Unfortunately two hungry calves can move faster than a middle-aged woman on a weight loss diet spying a cherry cobbler, so I seldom make it out before the head butting commences. Now that they know I can somehow provide the milk, they try and force more out of me with their foreheads. Usually all they get out of me however, is a few choice adjectives that I purposely save up for occasions such as this.

They always seem to manage to butt at least one of the bottles, which goes flying out of my hands. I learned very quickly, and I might add a little painfully, about the folly of bending over to pick up a dropped bottle. A rump in the air is like a butting beacon to a calf. In most cases it is the largest target in the vicinity and what he perceives is his best chance at making something happen. So I've actually become quite adept at kicking the bottle over the fence rather than picking it up because my ability to sit down again depends on it. I practice dropkicking and punting bottles in the yard year-around to hone my skills in anticipation of feeding calves.

If you, however, are not an accomplished bottle kicker, I would suggest taking off your shoe and picking the bottle up with your toes, duct taping magnets to the bottle and your wrist, tying a string to it to create a bottle yoyo or make sure you have a large supply of extra bottles so you can just leave them laying in the calf pen — anything to avoid bending over.

You would think that after awhile the calves would realize that no amount of head butting to my backside is going to turn the milk spigot on and that kneecaps don't make good pacifiers.

After several months of having the calves decorate my body with black and blue marks and being drenched in calf slobber, I began to wonder who would be ideally suited to bottle feed calves. I think the Michelin Man and the Stay Puff Marshmallow Man could be worthy contenders due to the extra padding they pack around. A sumi wrestler also comes to mind, as he would be hard for a couple of calves to push around. Wonder Woman could lasso the bottles with her golden rope and would never have to bend over…

But I guess when it comes right down to it, I still want to feed the calves myself because in spite of their head butting, slobbering and toe stomping, that split second that they look at me through long fluttering eyelashes as they wrap their necks around my legs and lean against me makes it all worthwhile…

95

" *The crop always seems better in our neighbor's field, and our neighbor's cow gives more milk.*"
Publius Ovidius Naso, known as Ovid

Gun Fever

While having dinner at a restaurant the other night, a friend of ours happened to mention that her guard dog, a Great Pyrenees/Akbash cross just had puppies. We were teeth deep into our steaks when she said to my husband, "You know, you guys could really use one of these dogs. You wouldn't ever have to worry about coyotes on your place again."

"I don't worry about coyotes now," said my husband. "I have a varmint rifle that sits by the door. I don't have to feed it; it only barks when I pull the trigger, and it doesn't poop."

"Which reminds me," he said as he turned to me.

I quickly tried to change the subject.

"Isn't this great flat iron steak?" I said. "Boy, what about those 49ers, I hear they're on a winning streak. Hey, did you know that farmers in England are required by law to provide their pigs with toys?"

But it was too late. His eyes were already glazing over and his upper lip was beginning to tremble with excitement. A faint layer of perspiration began to pool on his forehead and he was squinting down the upper tine of his fork drawing a bead on a bottle of Bud Light resting on a table across the restaurant.

"I could use another rifle," he said reluctantly letting the bottle slip from his fork sights as if to give the beer a reprieve. Fortunately he didn't get out the higher caliber steak knife or the double barrel spoon.

I ignored his comment hoping against all hope that he was merely having an intense craving for alcohol. But all the signs were there - the itchy trigger finger, the amnesia about how many guns he already owns, and incoherent babbling about how good the cattle market is expected to be this year. Yup, it was evident he had gun fever.

Unfortunately, the only known cure for gun fever is to buy guns and the recommended dosage depends largely on the size of the pocketbook and how well the afflicted can ignore the resistance offered by his wife. However, I suspect the medical professional who came up with this remedy owns shares in Remington and Winchester companies.

We made it through dinner and when he began telling the waitress how he could shoot a two-inch twig off of a tree in a snowstorm with 60 mile an hour winds, blindfolded, if only he had the Remington 40XRBR with a 2 oz. trigger, custom stock and Nikon Monarch 5-20x44SF riflescope, I knew it was time to take him home.

As soon as we got in the car he started mapping out for me where "we" could get his rifle, the best person to buy the custom stock from and a great discount warehouse for scopes.

He continued with his tangent, which sounded something like blah, blah, blah, ammunition, blah, blah, blah, barrels, blah, blah, blah, bluing, bullets, blah, blah, blah, cases, cleaning, gauges, and blah, blah, gunpowder. To me it all translated in to something along the lines of "Let's take all of the money we have and invest it in a mink farm."

After the 30-minute drive home I was exhausted and beaten. Nothing I had said, not even, "You'll shoot your eye out!" had any affect on him. He was so delirious with the fever that he even began talking about getting two varmint rifles, so he would have one for 500 yards and one for 1,000 yards.

"You can't even see something as small as a varmint at 1,000 yards!" I protested.

"Hellllloooooo," he said, "that's why I've been telling you we need to get two of the Nikon Monarch 5-20x44SF rifle scopes."

"O.K.," I finally gave in, "get your new rifle."

That was immediately followed by a glaring stare from him, the same kind of look a well-seasoned boxer gives his opponent before knocking him out of the ring.

"O.K.," I said, "get your *two* new rifles."

"Really!" he said. "You don't mind?"

"No, go ahead. Just tell me about how much it will cost," I said.

"Well," he said as he started mentally figuring the price of the rifles, custom stocks, after market triggers, scopes and reloading equipment, "it could be as high as $4,000 for everything."

"Fine," I said as I grabbed a mug of hot cider and sat down in front of the computer with a stack of mail order catalogs.

"What are doing?" he asked.

"I figured I better get started because it's going to take me awhile to decide what I want to get for $4,000," I said.

"What do you mean?" he said with a puzzled look.

"Well, I'm sure you want to be fair, don't you?" I asked. "If you are spending $4,000, then I should be able to spend that much, too, shouldn't I?"

Miraculously, like the dark clouds opening to reveal the light of the sun, the fever began to break.

"You know," he said, "I guess I don't really need those rifles after all. I already have one that seems to be doing the job. Besides we need to buy fertilizer this spring for the pastures and we do have a pretty high gas bill to pay this month."

"Yeah," I said, "you're right. It's a good thing you are so sensible when it comes to money or we'd be in debt up to our ears."

He smiled and leaned over and kissed me on the forehead before trotting up the stairs to bed.

I immediately grabbed a pen and paper and began to draft the following letter:

Dear members of the American Medical Association:

I, a mere rancher's wife, have single-handedly discovered a cure for a malady that has affected men since the mid 1200s when man first discovered that lit gunpowder could project a stone through the air. Yes, incredulous as it may seem, I have found a cure for gun fever....

Bruised and Battered
by Minerals

There was no tornado, for once a cow didn't run over me and I wasn't side swiped by a Volkswagen bus. Had one or any combination of those things happened to me, I would have at least had a good excuse for the battering I took last weekend that left me looking and feeling like I'd been prodded up the cattle chute five too many times.

Nope, I can't blame the beating I took from being in a natural disaster or even an unnatural one. I was physically abused by a 50-pound sack of livestock supplement. I know, as incredible as it may seem, I let a sack of highly palatable trace minerals and vitamins with the aroma cows love get the best of me.

One reason we are feeding our cows this supplement is because the sack says it is supposed to promote optimum body condition and reduce winter stress. I think they got it backwards because it actually reduced my body condition and promoted my optimum winter stress.

I picked up the unwieldy bag of minerals, which weighs almost half as much as me, and proceeded to take it out to the cows. I vaguely remember thinking, "I wonder why Mike, (my husband) had worn a path in the snow all along the edge of the fence to pack the minerals to the cows rather than cut across the middle of the field to the salt feeder?" Apparently, it was one of those thoughts where I decided I was just a little smarter than the average rancher and could save myself a few extra steps. I seem to have a lot of thoughts like that…

The snow was about two feet deep and had formed a hard crusty surface on top – or so I thought. I took about 10 steps and suddenly my feet went through the top layer of snow. I immediately fell to my hands and knees, and dropped the sack of minerals.

I was wearing insulated overalls, a down coat, heavy snow pack boots and thick mittens, which didn't allow much freedom of movement. I must have looked like a beached whale flopping around on the snow unable to bend at the knees and elbows. I finally wallowed around and made it back to my feet.

I have been told I'm stubborn and now I'm beginning to think there must be some truth to that, because I was even more determined to stay on the route that I had chosen rather than back up and follow the path already in place.

I tried it again, and again, and about every 10 steps I went through the top of the snow and fell to my knees dropping the bag of mineral.

I was so tired from repeatedly falling and picking up the bag that by the time I neared the feeder, I was on my belly pushing the bag across the snow in front of me. I had to flounder around on the ground with the bag for a good 10 minutes before I could muster the strength to lift it up completely over my head and into the feeder. Thank goodness the feeder is only about six inches off the ground or I never would have made it.

Fortunately, this mineral company makes their bags with a waterproof plastic coated lining. I'm guessing that must mean I'm not the only one to have wallowed one of their bags around in the snow. They must have crash test ranch wives, similar to the crash test dummies used in the auto industry to try out their products and determine what safety features are needed.

Unfortunately, although the bags are waterproof, it turns out those ranch wives doing the testing must have never tried to open the bags, or the company would have realized the need to come up with a better system. I have never pulled that stitched-in string at the top of a mineral bag or even a bag of dog food and had it work. Either the string breaks or it bunches into a knot. And yes, I've tried both ends. If the companies insist on using this method they need to attach a disposable seam ripper to every bag or at the least include a coupon to hire some help, perhaps the men who model for the covers of romance novels could use some extra work…

At any rate, this bag was no exception and after all the work of getting it to the feeder, I couldn't get it open. I dug through my pockets for a knife, but all I found was a hair barrette and a half eaten Ding Dong. I poked and prodded at the bag of minerals with my barrette until the barrette bent in two from the pressure, much like me.

I ripped at the bag with my fingernails, I kicked it with my boots, I cussed at it, but none of this helped, although the cussing did make me feel a little better. I scanned the pasture; there was no rock, stick or rodent in sight with large teeth so out of desperation I finally decided to gnaw on it myself.

I chewed on the bag like a rat after grain, and finally after several minutes, I managed to make a small hole, which I was able to enlarge enough with my fingers to finally spill out that precious mineral.

Yes, I had been battered and bruised by a bag of minerals, but on the bright side, after chewing the bag open, I'm pretty sure I don't have a selenium deficiency.

Family Cow Circle

5¢

How to tell if
your cow is sad

**Designer
Ear Tags**

Hay recipes!

**Finding the bull
of your dreams**

Women's Hog Journal

5¢

In this issue:
A healthy hog is a happy hog
Keeping a clean pig sty
Crafts your hogs will love!

The Romantic Rancher

Our good neighbor Billy Bob McKrackin is a rancher with a romantic soul. He says he has become an expert at finding ways to show his wife, Eunice, how much he loves her. While I was outside doing chores the other day, I saw Billy Bob and asked him what he did for Valentine's Day last week. He says he doesn't do anything special for this holiday. He says he prefers to show her how much he cares all the time rather than one day a year.

"My daddy was romantic and my granddaddy was romantic," says Billy Bob. "My grandma used to say if she had as much romance in her little finger as granddaddy had in his whole body, she would have more than enough... or was it not enough... maybe it was granddaddy who had it in his finger. Oh well, you get the idea, we McKrackins are a romantic bunch – it's in our blood."

Billy Bob says part of being romantic is finding out what your missus really likes. "Once in awhile Eunice will try to tell me she would like to have some of those pretty dangly things to hang in her ears, but I know that's not true," he says. "One time I got the cow ear tag gun out and tried to put a pair of number 2s in her lobes and she wouldn't have no part of it. She said first of all she didn't want to be number 2. I told her if she just waited awhile I thought old number 4 would be rubbing her tags off on the fence any day now and she could have those. Like I said, when it came right down to it, she really didn't want dangly things hanging from her ears.

Eunice is more of a meat and potatoes kind of gal, Billy Bob says.

"Oh, you mean you take her out to dinner?" I ask.

"Nah, I mean I give her meat and potatoes," he says. "Yesiree, just give her a seven pound rump roast and a gunnysack of spuds and watch her eyes light up. She gets so excited she starts waving the frying pan around and yells, 'Here, let me give you something for all your trouble.'

"Shoot, I tell her she doesn't need to give me anything — nothin' 'cept a hunk of that rump roast for dinner. More than once in her excitement she has lost her grip on that frying pan and hit me square on the noggin. Course she always apologizes by saying I'm lucky she didn't hit me harder. Eunice is like that — polite and all."

"Well, do you ever give her something that hasn't been previously used by a cow or that she doesn't have to cook?" I ask.

"Oh, sure," he says. "Once in awhile I surprise her with some of those girly magazines she likes. You know *Women's Hog Journal, Ladies Home Tractor, Family Cow Circle* and the like.

Course it depends on whether Billy Jr. is with me when I go to the recycling center. If I hold him up by his ankles he can reach way down into those recycle bins and fish out some that still have the covers on. And if they're dirty, ol' Elroy our dog licks 'em clean on the way home so they're pert near good as new when Eunice gets 'em."

"And sometimes I give her flowers," he says. "But she says she spends all summer watering and weeding them and I should leave her flower garden alone. I guess she thinks I'm spoiling her too much and should let her pick them herself."

"I see. What kinds of romantic things do you do that don't involve giving her something?" I ask.

"Well, let me think a minute," he says. "There was the time I stripped down to my undershorts and suspenders and danced for her. I sang that song by that McGraw feller. 'I like it, I love it, I want some more of it.' I mean to tell you, the sight of me shimmying and crooning sent chills up and down her spine. She got so cold from those chills she slept in her longjohns with the little footies in them for the better part of a week — and it was the middle of summer. She kept saying, 'don't even think about coming near me.' I guess it was just too much for her. I tend to have that effect on women."

"See, I just moved like this," he demonstrated as he danced around the barnyard in his Carhartt overalls. He stopped and looked at me. "Did I just see you shiver?"

"Billy Bob, it's only 20 degrees out here," I said as I rolled my eyes.

"Yup, I still got it," he says, "it's almost a sin to have this much romance oozing outta one man."

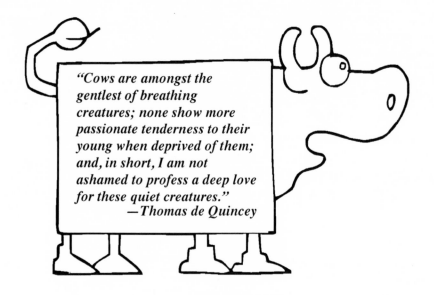

"Cows are amongst the gentlest of breathing creatures; none show more passionate tenderness to their young when deprived of them; and, in short, I am not ashamed to profess a deep love for these quiet creatures."
—Thomas de Quincey

Shoot Fire And The Large
Canine-Like Animal

Our neighbor Billy Bob McKrackin had a run-in with wolves one night last week. Fortunately his dog "Shoot Fire" warned him — well sort of — that there was a wolf in the barnyard. I say "sort of" because even though Shoot Fire can normally put up a loud enough ruckus to raise the dead, on this occasion he crept silently into the bedroom and whispered in Billy Bob's ear.

Eunice, Billy Bob's wife, was the first to hear Shoot Fire's hoarse "psssst." Never having heard a dog whisper, Eunice wasn't sure what it was. At first she thought Billy Bob's indigestion was getting the best of him, but she didn't detect any odor, which always followed his body noises. She sat up in bed and saw Shoot Fire pssssting in Billy Bob's ear.

About that time Billy Bob opened his eyes and saw bulging brown orbs and a weird little toothy grin about two inches from his face. He was startled by the face — Shoot Fire's — not Eunice's. He had become accustomed to Eunice's curlers and nightly mudpack routine years ago.

Billy Bob yelped, which scared Shoot Fire who dove under the bed. Now wide-awake he could hear the commotion going on outside with cattle bawling and horses running.

Billy Bob jumped out of bed and into his suspender drawers. He ran outside and saw a wolf running around the barnyard harassing and nipping at the livestock.

By this time Eunice, suspecting there was a racoon after her chickens, ran to the door with the .30 -.30 rifle. Shoot Fire, with a sudden burst of courage, bolted out the door between Eunice's legs and took off after the wolf.

Billy Bob knew that the dog was no match for a wolf so tried to get the dog to come back. He was standing in the middle of the barnyard yelling, "Shoot Fire!, Shoot Fire!" hoping the dog would retreat before it was too late.

Eunice, still in a sleep-induced fog, thought Billy Bob was yelling at her so she raised the rifle to her shoulder and squeezed the trigger.

Knowing that Eunice wasn't the best shot, Billy Bob hit the dirt and looked up just in time to see the wolf fall over dead.

"Good shot, Mama," he yelled to Eunice. Eunice, not one to shy away from taking the credit, didn't bother to tell Billy Bob that she was trying to hit a skunk that was creeping along the fence line toward the chicken coop about 10 feet to the right of the wolf.

Shoot Fire, seizing the opportunity, went after the dead animal with a vengeance chewing its ears and tearing into its hide.

Billy Bob had to literally pry Shoot Fire off the wolf to get him to go back inside so they could all get some sleep.

The next morning a biologist with the Oregon Department of Fish and Wildlife showed up on the McKrackin's porch.

"Good morning," he said, "I was driving through the area and noticed a large canine-like animal lying out there in your barnyard."

"You mean that wolf?" asked Billy Bob.

"Well, I can't say for sure that's a wolf until we get a DNA test and have a team of at least seven university experts come out and identify the animal, but if it is, did you know that wolves are endangered?"

Billy Bob said, "That wolf's not in danger any more, it's deader 'n a door nail."

"No, I mean it's listed as an endangered species and there is a $100,000 fine for anyone who kills one," said the biologist.

Billy Bob thinking fast and remembering how Shoot Fire had chewed the wolf up the night before quickly replied, "Well, that may be, but my dog killed it – twern't nothing I could do!"

"I did see where it was chewed up some, but I also noticed there was a bullet lodged in its skull," said the biologist.

"The dog chewed it up so bad," said Billy Bob rather pleased with himself at thinking so quickly on his feet, "that I had to shoot it to put it out of its misery. I can't stand to see a poor animal suffer."

"Boy, I'd like to see the dog that could take down an animal like that," said the biologist.

"Sure thing," said Billy Bob. "Shoot Fire," he yelled. Eunice immediately appeared at the door with the .30-.30.

No, no," said Billy Bob, "the dog, get the dog."

Reluctantly, Eunice set the rifle down and fetched Shoot Fire.

Now Billy Bob, although quick on his feet, hadn't thought this one through very well.

Shoot Fire, never very good with strangers, came tearing out the door and grabbed the biologist by the pant leg, pulling and snarling for all he was worth, which wasn't very much because Shoot Fire is a Chihuahua...

"I think we have a problem here," said the biologist looking down at the little dog. "This dog couldn't have possibly killed that animal."

"Just supposing he didn't," said Billy Bob, "is there any law that specifically says you can't kill a large canine-like animal?"

"Well, no," said the biologist, "but I think we both really know what kind of animal..."

Billy Bob cut him off, "I know no such thing, if a man schooled in wildlife such as yourself can't say for sure it's a wolf, how in the heck would I know?"

It's All About The Water

Anyone who knows anything about ranching on pasturelands knows it's not about the cattle, it's not about the hay or crops, it's not even about galloping horses on green meadows — ranching is all about the water. Without the water, there is no ranch.

That's why ranchers become very uptight when the rivers full from the spring thaw begin to dwindle down to a slow trickle toward the end of summer. This time of year they are trying to squeeze every last drop of water out of the ditch and force it onto the grass.

In fact if it rains one fraction of one/bazillionth of an inch, the equivalent of about five drops, ranchers think they've had a real soaker and call the watermaster to make sure all that "extra" water is in their ditch. Even if it only sends a half-inch dribble onto the grass for two seconds, during those two seconds they are in irrigator's Heaven.

Some ranchers get their children involved in getting water on the grass. One such ploy is to purchase the large super soaker squirt guns and get them to have a water fight out in the middle of a pasture. Of course this only works if you set them up to refill the guns out of a neighbor's ditch —one who has better water rights.

Although it's not quite the right type of water, some ranchers even resort to sabotaging the toilets in the house this time of year and telling everyone in the family they will have to go outside. Of course by outside, they mean hop on the four-wheeler and drive to a dry spot in the cow pasture. These ranchers also tend to stock up on extra soda this time of year to "inspire" the need to "go" more often.

When water gets short some ranchers who irrigate with sprinklers conveniently ignore a sprinkler bird for a couple of days when it falls off and creates an extra gusher of water. When a riser (where the water enters the sprinkler pipes) blows it spews a gusher similar to an uncapped city fire hydrant. Blown risers can go unnoticed for several days if a rancher puts out a roadblock to keep his neighbors from driving by.

A lot of ranchers plan their vacations in late summer just about the time the water gets short. They generally travel just far enough away that their cell phones are out of range so the watermaster can't reach them to tell them to shut their water off.

Some ranchers will resort to rain dances and surprisingly they have had some success, especially when they "accidentally" kick open a ditch headgate during their precipitation boogie.

Unexplained, almost supernatural, things happen on ranches during times of water shortages. Big wads of sod mysteriously fall into ditches to back up water for irrigating. Rocks get piled neatly in places that divert water onto someone's property. Boards are taken out of ditch boxes that regulate the water during the night and then are miraculously back in place in the morning. Irrigation dams that ranchers could have sworn they took out of the ditch somehow end up in the ditch again. Since ranchers seem to have no idea how these things happen, it's usually blamed on the cows.

Ranchers spend days going over property boundaries and water rights. They have been known to redo an entire fence line if it will get them five inches more of property with better water rights. And if water allocated to that five inches happens to spread into the next 40 acres, oh well, that's just the way it goes....

Over the years, ranchers have invented all kinds of elaborate measuring devices to ensure they are getting all of the water they are entitled to. Our neighbor, Billy Bob McKrackin, does it the old fashioned way. He just takes a wild guess, usually in his favor. When a more accurate measurement is called for he uses a complicated method consisting of a tree branch and a waterproof marking pen. When he needs to be even more accurate than that, he sticks his boot clad foot in the ditch and measures how close it comes to his knee.

To regulate water Billy Bob places a car door in the main ditch that flows onto his property. When the watermaster asks him to turn his water down, he complies by saying he will crank the water down two turns. Of course what he means is that he cranked the window on the car door down two turns and actually got more water, but it sounds like he's doing it right.

Billy Bob's wife, Eunice, has learned not to have her hair done this time of year because going to town in a car with no doors can really mess up a good do.

Billy Bob had a run in with Tom, the local deputy watermaster, the other day. Tom told him he was going to have to come up with a better system than car doors and sticks to regulate and measure his water.

"I've been using the same system for 40 years," said Billy Bob. "Well, almost the same. The first 20 years they were Packard doors and now I'm using Ford. But they work just the same."

"I'm sorry Billy Bob," said Tom. "But times have changed and everyone wants to know exactly how much water you are getting — in inches — not in pert near to my knee, second notch on the stick or window crank measurements."

"But I'm getting exactly what I have always gotten – not near enough," said Billy Bob.

"That may be," said Tom. "But if we had a better measuring system, we'd know for sure."

Billy Bob, always one to comply with the local authorities, put in a whole new system. It consisted of 2x4s with a ruler drawn on them and small sliding house windows. Eunice was able to have her hair done again, but had to start taking her baths in the afternoon because the holes in the bathroom wall were a little too chilly in the mornings.

Tom wasn't much happier with Billy Bob's new system, and shortly after this incident announced his retirement.

Bad Bart Gets the Boot

If our black Angus bull, Bart, were a person he'd be like one of those gun-slinging outlaws from the movies who could simultaneously shoot a man in the back while charming the ladies.

In his short life, he's nearly 2 years old; he has already gained a reputation on our place. When we turned him in with the cows and other bulls for the first time this summer he acted like the new guy in prison. He immediately went over to the biggest 4-year-old bull we have and head butted him. A fight ensued, and what Bart lacked in size and experience he made up for in persistence. He eventually wore the other bull down until he tired of the struggle and walked away. Needless to say the cows swoon over him — the bulls avoid him.

Bart has the typical bad boy story. He started life as an orphan. He didn't know his father, he could have been any one of about 10 bulls and of course none of those bulls owned up to it. Shortly after birth his mom was taken away to another pasture by mistake, anyway that's what we were told. We have to wonder if perhaps his mother just left him for greener pastures and that's the story his previous owner told him to spare his feelings.

At some point Bart will probably have to go on the Montel Williams show or Oprah to find out who his true father is. As usually happens on those shows, I'm sure there will be a big scene with lots of denial on the dad's part — "she's out in the pasture with 10 other bulls, how do you know it was me? Bart doesn't even look like me, he has a small head and beady eyes." And then there will be lots of crying when Bart's dad is backed into a corner and made to realize that the DNA tests don't lie, and he will have to start paying child support or in Bart's case, share some grass.

At any rate, Bart was smaller than the other bulls and obviously picked on during his first few months of life, as evidenced by his surly attitude. His smaller size, however is what attracted us to him, because being smaller, he was also cheaper.

We started feeding Bart grain when he was a youngster and thus got to know him quite well. He was corralled with another young bull, Bert. Every time we grained them Bart would spend about 15 minutes trying to run Bert away from the feed bunk. Consequently Bart grew like a weed since he was eating the amount of grain meant for two bulls. Bert unfortunately became an underachiever with low self-esteem and rather than go out into the pasture with the cows and be further subjected to Bart and the other bulls, he went to the livestock sale where he sold his body to the highest bidder — a sad, but all too common story.

When we were graining Bart, we made the mistake of scratching his back one day. After that, he insisted that we scratch it every day. He always started out nice, like a puppy wanting a pat on the head, but his mild demeanor always deteriorated rather rapidly. He would lower his head and place it against one of our knees. We thought, "how cute!" and would continue scratching.

His thoughts, however, were more along the lines of "Let me remind you who is in charge." After a few minutes of scratching, he would get this funny look in his eyes and cock his head sideways similar to the way John Wayne looked when he swaggered into a bar full of outlaws. Bart would start pressing against our knees with his head, lightly at first, and then not so lightly. Before we knew what was happening, he would shove us a couple of feet forward, grin, dance around for a minute, and then want his back rubbed more.

Even so, his actions were still kind of cute, but we knew we couldn't let him get away with it at 400 pounds because soon he would weigh 2,000 pounds and it wouldn't be so cute any more. So every time he started pushing against our knees we gave him a light rap on the nose with the heel of our boots. He quickly got to where every time he would see us begin to raise our foot, he would immediately stop pushing, uncock his head and his eyes would return to normal.

Now Bart is almost full-grown and every time we go out into the pasture to check the cows he comes running up to us to have his back scratched. It is always a little alarming at first to see a 2,000-pound animal running toward you. But even at his size, Bad Bart — the bull that can easily put three bulls that outweigh him by 200 pounds in their place and barrel through a barbed wire fence like it wasn't even there — still cringes at the sight of a raised boot.

After Bart finds out who his real father is, he will have to visit with Dr. Phil to find out why he recoils from a boot. "Is it any boot, Bart, or just the lizard skin Tony Lamas? Is this boot problem the truth you believe about yourself when no one else is looking? How's that working for you?"

"*Parties who want milk should not seat themselves on a stool in the middle of the field in hopes that the cow will back up to them.*"
Elbert Hubbard

Ranching with Peter Sellers

What does Peter Sellers have to do with fences, you might ask. Well, for those of you who don't know of the late actor, Sellers was the bumbling Inspector Clouseau who starred in the Pink Panther movie series. He had a unique way of pronouncing common words. For instance instead of phone he said "pheone," you was "yeuw," and solved was "sol-ved."

Any person who did not understand his dialect, Clouseau referred to them as a fool or an idiot. And to reflect anger or dissatisfaction with something Clouseau always added the word "swine" before it, as in "swine parrot," "swine moat."

We had a Pink Panther marathon this last month, watching all of the movies in the series, and apparently it affected us more than we realized.

My 20-something son, Jake, and I were out fixing fences the other day. He was walking along the fence line and I was flanking him with the four-wheeler full of tools. We came to an irrigation ditch and he said, "There's a bimp."

I said, "A what?"

He repeated, "A bimp."

I looked in the direction he was looking and said, "Oh, you mean a bump."

He said, assuming the Inspector Clouseau character, "That's what I have been saying you fool!"

I drove the four-wheeler through the ditch, which was rather deep, and received a chiropractic adjustment to my spine in the process.

"Swine bimp," I said, "it's deeper than I thought."

"Yes, I kneuw that... I kneuw that" said Jake.

From then on that day everything was a swine including "swine hammer," "swine wire stretchers," and "swine post" as we "rahpaired" the fence. And of course we both couldn't tell each other anything without saying, "I kneuw that."

Needless to say, Inspector Clouseau spent the day with us.

At one point my cell phone rang and it was for Jake.

"The pheone is for you," I said.

"The what?" he asked.

"The pheone," I said holding it out to him.

"You mean the phone?" he said.

"Yes, that's what I've been saying you fool!"

"I kneuw that," he said. "I will rahceive it now."

Gradually Inspector Clouseau faded, but during the week other actors cropped up.

While we were spraying thistles the Governor of California and ex-actor Arnold Schwarzenegger paid a visit.

As we sprayed the thistles they got a hardy dose of 2-4D and a "hasta la vista baby" along with an occasional "I'll be back!" if it was a really big stickery one.

Clint Eastwood even popped in with "Do you feel lucky?' Well, do ya punk?" Apparently the thistles didn't feel very lucky because they shriveled as we sprayed them.

One day while we were working on the fence Jake stopped to look out over the pasture and the Looney Tunes showed up.

"What are you doing?" I asked.

"Hunting wascally wabbits, be vewwy vewwy quiet," he replied.

"I think it's duck season, Elmer," I said.

"I thought there was something very scwewy around here," he said.

"Besides, you don't have any bullwets," I reminded him.

"Well, what do you know, no bullwets," he said as he turned walking back toward the house.

"Where are you going?" I yelled after him.

"For some west and wewaxation at wast!" he said

"What a revolting development this is," I said in my best Daffy Duck voice. "What about the fence?"

He didn't respond so I tried a little Foghorn Leghorn, "Pay attention to me boy - I'm not just talkin' to hear my head roar!"

Turns out he just went to get a jug of water and returned with his pu36 explosive space modulator. Actually it was a roast beef sandwich, but as Marvin the Martian, he had to make do on his threat to blow the fence up because he said, "It obstructs my view of Venus."

He pointed his sandwich at the fence, and like Marvin, said, "Where's the kaboom? There was supposed to be an Earth-shattering kaboom!"

Just then a black ball of fur came flying through the air and grabbed his pu36 modulator. It wasn't the kaboom he expected, it was Puddin' Head, our black lab, Lord only knows what cross dog.

"Oh, that wasn't a bit nice...You have made me very angry... very angry indeed!" said Jake still in his Marvin the Martian character.

Puddin' just looked at him and wagged her tail, happy that she was able to save the fence from being disintegrated and get a tasty snack at the same time.

Changing roles to Yosemite Sam Jake said, "You ornery fur-bearin' rebel, you'll pay for this! I'm the roughest, toughest he-man hombré that's ever crossed the Rio Grande. An' I ain't no namby-pamby."

I looked at Puddin' and then at Jake. "I believe th-th-th-th-that's all, Folks!" I said. "We've got to get back to rahparing this swine fence."

"Yes, I kneuw that... I kneuw that" said Jake.

The Tractor Road Less Traveled Leads To Dinner Out

One of the first things a rancher's wife learns is how to drive the tractor. So if you are a woman enamored with the idea of leading a home, home on the range lifestyle with long days of riding horses through cattle and antelope, and think you can obtain it by marrying a rancher, you better think twice. It's more like home, home, in the fields where the John Deere and the Massey Fergusons play.

I'm not saying that you don't get an opportunity to ride horses and work with the cattle, but that usually comes only after you've spent hours bouncing around in a tractor seat while plowing, disking, swathing, raking or baling hay, pulling a feed wagon or harrowing fields. And of course by then, with tractor tush setting in, you aren't too keen about getting on a horse anyway.

I recently had an opportunity to take my tractor driving to new heights of ecstasy. I had to drive it home from town where it was in the shop for repairs. That doesn't sound like a big chore, but when you consider it takes the better part of a day to drive the 25-mile distance, it is both a mind and butt numbing experience.

When my husband dropped me off at the tractor shop for the drive home, I asked him if it had enough diesel in it.

"Yes, it has plenty," he said as he rolled his eyes at my inquiry.

"How do you know without checking," I said because the gas gauge hasn't worked on the tractor for several years.

"I know, it's fine," he said, "now stop fussing and hurry up so you can get home in time for dinner." Dinner? It was only 9 a.m., so now I was the one rolling my eyes.

"Maybe we can go out for dinner tonight?" I ventured... thinking I'd be tired after spending so much of the day in the tractor.

"Nah, when I get home I'll take a roast out of the freezer for you to cook tonight," he said.

Rats!

Knowing that it would be a long journey, I had prepared for the tractor trip. I brought food and drinks, laptop computer, camera, cards for solitaire, blanket and pillow, extra change of clothes...

The first thing I discovered is that even though you are going unbelievably slow in a tractor down the highway, you can't type on a computer and drive at the same time. For one thing with such a bouncy seat, you can't keep the laptop on your lap. And the tractor won't steer itself. Oh, and you kind of have to watch where you are going, there's always that to contend with.

Unfortunately those little problems took care of any ideas of taking a nap too. And getting waved at with the middle finger three times in the first half-mile by people passing me in automobiles didn't give me much confidence in my ability to play solitaire while driving.

But, there was always the radio… And if I could actually have heard it over the sound of the tractor engine and the big wheels rotating on pavement, it would have been much easier to listen to.

I tried singing, but even I can't listen to myself for very long without wondering where that talent took a nosedive in my family's gene pool.

Along the way, I did however invent what I think would be a wonderful new video game called "Tractor Sideswipe." The idea is to see how many mailboxes you can hit with a tractor, or how many you can avoid. I decided to wait and see how well I did on my journey before committing to hitting the mailboxes or missing the mailboxes for the game.

I went through all of my food in the first three hours and was just about on my second bottle of water when a realization hit me. I'm not exactly pulling a porta-potty with me and there is no public bathroom for miles, actually none on my route unless you count the occasional large tree or abandoned barn. So I decided I better take it easy on the drinks.

Just about the time I was thinking it would be more fun to watch grass grow than drive a tractor home, the engine started to sputter. I pulled over to the side of the road as far as I could get, which means I was still covering most of one lane. The tractor died so I started it up again. It seemed to be running so I gave it some throttle and took off again.

About one quarter-mile down the road it started sputtering again so I pulled over a second time. This time it died and I couldn't get it started again. Fortunately I had my cell phone so I called my husband.

"What's wrong with it?" he asked.

"It died and won't start again," I replied.

He went through the usual check list… did you give it some throttle… did you turn off the choke after you got a little ways down the road... did you turn the key when tried to start it... did you push in the clutch...

I replied an exasperated "yes" to all of the above.

A few minutes and about seven middle finger waves from passing motorists later, he arrived in his pickup and popped the hood and started checking things out. He fiddled with wires, pulled dipsticks out and tightened cables. I was still sitting in the tractor cab so he asked me to try starting it again.

It made a halfhearted attempt to engage the pistons and then died. My husband went around to the back of his pickup and emerged with a gas can full of diesel.

I swung open the door of the tractor cab and started to go into the I told you so routine, but thought better of it...

"Dinner out tonight?" I asked.

"I guess so," he said without looking up from pouring the diesel into the tank.

In the News

Rebel Cows Go on Rampage

In a startling turn of events, cows that were being herded to greener pastures through Baker City's downtown area became highly agitated and a bovine riot ensued. Onlookers said it was the strangest and most terrifying thing they have ever seen.

As dairy farmer Wayne Brown and his stockdogs, Fluffy and Fifi, maneuvered the 75 cows down Main Street, the lead cow, Daisy, bolted through the window at Manny's House of

Bread. Other cows followed. They trashed the bakery overturning mixers, stomping on eggs and powdering their noses with flour.

As the cows retreated they took several items including milk, butter and cream. Manny and his wife, Whyme were shaken, but unharmed.

The cows continued their rampage bursting through doors at Coldson's Ice Cream Parlor where they dumped out vats of caramel and chocolate fudge sauce. Before fleeing with hooves full of ice cream tubs, they stuffed cherries up Iamso Coldson's nose and in his ears.

Coldson said the cherries were fairly easy to retrieve, but he didn't think he would be able to serve them to his customers. He estimated the damage and loss to his inventory at somewhere around "a bazillion dollars."

"It was almost like they were taking back their milk products," said Marvin Steponme, owner of the local Sugarhigh Candy Shoppe. "They came in and went straight for the Milk Duds. I've never seen anything like it!"

Other businesses hit by the rebel cows included the Cheese Whiz, Dairy Princess and Pizza Smut.

The Baker City Police Department was called in an effort to stop the cow rampage, but their hands were tied.

"Cows have the right-of-away on public lands," said Lt. Roger That. "There was nothing we could do."

After the cows settled down, a visibly embarrassed Brown and his dogs managed to round them up and head them down the street again.

Once the cows reached the pasture, they feasted on their stolen loot, which included chocolate milk, milk chocolate candy, strawberry ice cream, and cheese pizza. Soon after, Brown was cited for excessive cow flatulence and fined $265.24 per cow.

You Can Ride Hard, But You Can't Put Your Animal Away Wet

Local horse owners will no longer be able to ride their horses hard and put them away wet thanks to a new law just passed in Baker County.

"The next horse I see that's been rode hard and put away wet, someone's going to get a big fine," said Baker Sheriff Dudley Monighan. Monighan said the enforcement of this law is long overdue.

The law states that horse owners can still ride their animals hard, but they have to be completely dry before they put them away. This law also applies to mules, donkeys, zebras, camels and large dogs.

However, Monighan said these animals could still be rode easy and put away wet. Or they can be worked on the ground hard and put away wet as long as you don't ride them. Another option would be to ride them semi-hard and put them away almost wet.

After all, he said, "We don't want to take away all of their wet – dry options. We have to be reasonable."

Monighan said extra duty deputies would be put on patrol to monitor the hardness ridden and the wetness of an animal when they are put away.

"We have meters that will measure the moisture content of an animal's fur and deputies will be specially trained in how to determine when an animal is rode hard," he said. The deputies will receive this training at the "School of Hard Riding /Knocks" sometime in May.

"It's time we put an end to this practice and this tired old cliché," said Monighan.

Dogs Not to Run at Any Size

Along with dogs not being able to run at large, Baker City Police recently announced that dogs can no longer run at small or medium either.

"We want to send the message that dogs can no longer run at any size in our community," said Police Chief Richard Anderson.

Maxine Dunflop, a local resident said, "I don't like the new law one bit! My dogs have been able to run at small and medium for all of the 30 years I've lived here. It was bad enough they couldn't run at large, and now this."

Anderson said the new law will prevent owners of dogs that run at large from being discriminated against since it will encompass other sizes as well, and it will also save valuable police man hours.

"It has been very time consuming for our patrol officers to determine what size a dog is actually running at," he said. "There is currently no equipment available to determine this so what it boils down to is that we have just been taking our best guess as to how large they were running. Now, with this new law, we won't have to make that determination. Almost any dog that is running will be at small, medium or large."

With an increase in the popularity of Chihuahuas, Anderson said they might also add that dogs can no longer be allowed to run at tiny.

Town Upset Over Street Signs

Residents of the rural eastern Oregon town of Dawdle, are up in arms about streets signs that the Oregon Department of Transportation (ODOT) recently installed. The bright yellow signs have black lettering with the words "Slow Children."

Several parents in the community have expressed their dislike of the signs, which are placed at the beginning of every road leading into town. There are three roads that lead into Dawdle.

"We know we may not have the fastest children around," said Naomi Sloth. "My son, Claude isn't going to win a marathon, but he can keep up."

Residents say they don't know what prompted ODOT to put up the signs.

"Maybe they saw our children running in the school playground at recess and thought they were slower than normal," said parent, Peter Turtle. "But that's not fair to make that assumption without at least timing them in a 100-yard dash."

Twelve-year-old Jessica Slowerthanmolasses said she is highly offended by the implications of the signs.

"I've run with kids in nearby towns and they aren't any faster than I am," she said. "In fact I beat one kid. He had a broken leg, but it was in a walking cast so that doesn't count."

Parents are planning to protest at some point by picketing a nearby ODOT office.

"We've had one meeting since the signs were put up eight months ago and hope to have another one to organize the protest, as soon as we can get around to it," said Turtle.

ODOT official, Jim Runlikethewind, said, "We felt we needed to let tourists know that Dawdle has slow kids to hopefully avoid any accidents. I almost hit a little boy when I was driving through town because he didn't get out of my way fast enough."

Runlikethewind said ODOT doesn't plan to remove the signs. He said they are currently working on signs that say "Slow Parents" and "Slow Pets" that they hope to have in place by the end of the year."

"The town's dogs are almost slower than their kids," said Runlikethewind. "And since it's been proven that slowness is hereditary, we decided to put up signs to protect the parents as well."

Citizens Accuse Local Weather Forecasters of Being Unpredictable

Baker County citizens have filed complaints to the National Oceanic and Atmospheric Administration accusing local weather forecasters of being unpredictable.

Myron Meeks of Baker City said, "On Tuesday night they said it was going to rain Wednesday morning so I canceled my golf game. Turns out it was a really nice sunny day so I ended up working when I could have been hitting the greens."

Meeks and 12 others signed the complaints, which went out yesterday morning, stating, "We are tired of not being able to make plans because we can't trust the weather forecasts." They contend local forecasters can't tell the difference between a cumulus cloud and a stratus cloud, and wouldn't know a tsunami from a tornado if it swept through their house.

Local Meteorologist Les Muggy admits sometimes they are inaccurate, but says they aren't entirely to blame.

"We have outdated equipment and Roger Breezy, our rooftop observer, doesn't see as well as he used to." Breezy is 83, and Muggy said by the time he makes it to the top of the building the storm has usually passed over anyway.

Muggy said they also use the older style Dupler Radar, which can give false readings, instead of the newer Doppler.

He said due to the office's location next to the City sewer lagoon, they can't always smell the rain before it comes and they don't receive a very clear signal of the local weather channel.

However, they are trying out a new system called the Beasley Barometer that will ensure their weather predictions are more accurate. When they think it might rain, they will have Mrs. Beasley, who lives near the weather office, hang her laundry out on the line to dry to make sure it does indeed rain.

"We hope to have this system in place next week," Muggy said. Other plans, he said, include looking out the window more often and holding a wet finger up to see which direction the wind is blowing.

Journalist Arrested For Writing Crimes

A journalist and writer for rural eastern Oregon's Daily Drivel, Michael Michaels was taken into custody and arrested before being charged with 5,000 counts of reoccurring redundancy. The charge states that he has intentionally and knowingly repeatedly, time and time again, used verbose or unnecessary repetition in expressing ideas and comments in his newspaper articles. He was also charged with 3,000 counts of illegally using adverbs to modify his lively adjectives.

Michaels' trial was held Wednesday in the Baker County Circuit Court with Judge Beaker presiding. Beaker said Michaels' crimes are the most blatant misuse of the English language that he has seen to date.

When cross examining for the prosecution, District Attorney Henry Hansen, asked Michaels, "Everyone knows that glue is adhesive, so why did you use the term 'adhesive glue' in your article about the school children's art project?"

"Well," answered Michaels, "there are many different levels of sticky tacky adhesive bonding pastes and glues, and I wanted readers to know this was definitely the adhesive kind of glue."

Hansen continued, "Why did you state 'the flower opened up its smooth pink petals and bloomed, spreading its silken fingers to the shining sun?'

Surely you know, Mr. Michaels, smooth and silken have the same meaning, and when a flower opens its petals it is blooming? Furthermore, in the context you used the word 'fingers', it means virtually the same thing as petals. And what else would the sun be doing, but shinning?"

Michaels' obviously shaken by the DAs implications broke down and sobbed crying. Through intermittent and occasional watery tears he confessed.

"I know it was not right, in fact it was wrong of me to write those repeatedly redundant and ornately flowery items for the newspaper periodical publication I work for that employs me," he said. "But I have a minimum of the least amount of words I can use in an article, a word quota to meet, and sometimes I run out of actual real information and have to substitute replacement words in order to satisfy and please my editor. Besides, I'm being paid $1 per word. Why wouldn't I be wordy and like, redundant?"

At that point Judge Beaker slammed down his gavel.

"Although this court finds you guilty of grossly misusing the English language in your speech as well, that is not yet considered a crime. However for your written crimes, I hereby sentence you to five years of covering the Baker City Council meetings for the Daily Drivel and three years of writing obituaries.

Upon hearing the sentencing of what some later reported as unusually cruel, unkind and harsh treatment, Michaels swooned, collapsed, fell down and fainted.

Finally on Common Ground

My husband and I have found that as we grow older, we have more and more in common —especially our aches and pains.

It hasn't always been that way though. When we were married more than 20 years ago I was the cultured city gal and he was a genuine country boy. At times, the differences in our societal upbringings were… let's say… interesting.

For instance, I was used to staying up late at night and getting up around 8ish. He went to bed early and got up early.

We continued the different bedtime routines with me staying up late and him going to bed early for several years until his jumping up and down on the bed and whistling at an annoyingly high-pitched tone at 5 a.m. every morning finally wore me down. I had to go to bed earlier to get some sleep!

These days, we both go to bed around 8 p.m. with the guise of reading for a while. Within 15 minutes we are slumped over in a semi-comatose state and spend the next hour jerking awake every time we start to fall over. Finally, when the clock ticks to 9:30, a respectable bedtime hour, we both act like we have been awake the whole time and now it's time to actually go to sleep.

The main problem with this system is that it takes us months to finish a book. We are known at the local library as the "perpetual book re-newers." We have their phone number on speed dial.

Horses were another area where we differed. Growing up with them, he was an expert rider and incorporated them into his daily routines. He rode young, high-spirited horses with lots of get up and go, which he trained to turn on a dime. He very seldom engaged them in anything less than a full gallop, while skillfully straddling them with the ease of someone sitting in a BarcaLounger.

In contrast, I hadn't had much experience with horses. Shortly after we were married I was introduced to a 20-year-old horse, named "Asbestos" that was deemed "safe" for me to ride. When Asbestos trotted, which wasn't very often because he was more interested in eating grass, I hung on for dear life with about as much finesse as a black bear on a gymnast's balance beam.

However, to my credit, I could make fairly sharp turns with Asbestos – I hopped off and led him by his reins to get him pointed in the direction I wanted to go and then climbed back on.

Of course someone always has to bring up the rear when herding cattle, but I took that to new levels. Usually by the time I got my horse saddled and made it out into the pasture to help round up cattle, everyone was on their way back. And once anyone or anything – the dog, a goat, a duck, a low flying plane —was headed remotely in the direction of the barn Asbestos took that as his cue to head there as well, and there was no stopping him.

Although I never did master the equine sport, I am just happy I survived it! These days though, being a little older and a little stiffer in the joints, it isn't a problem — we both ride four-wheelers. I really like the idea of having brakes and he likes the idea of not having to bend over to shoe them.

Cows, of course have always been second nature to my husband. He seems to know what they are thinking, what they are about to do and what they are capable of doing if pushed in the right or wrong direction.

I on the other hand, having only seen cows in pastures while driving down the highway, had a lot to learn. It took me two years after we were married to finally figure out the difference between a heifer and a Hereford.

When it came to herding them, I was like the proverbial bad dog, always standing in the right gate at the wrong time or the wrong gate at the right time.

In those early years I tried to treat the cows like the cocker spaniels that I had previously owned. I quickly learned that even if you can get close enough, cows don't particularly like being petted on the head. They also won't come when you call them, could care less about a tasty snack (I tried giving them carrots and chocolate several times to no avail), and are prone to temper tantrums, especially if you keep chasing them around trying to cram a Hershey's Kiss in their mouth.

These days, I would like to think that I have learned the basics of the Tao of cow, but every once in awhile I still catch myself trying to pet one on the head.

We also had other minor differences that we have managed to work out over the years.

For example, when we were first married I wondered whose turn it was to cook dinner each night. Now I know it's always my turn.

He often wondered whose turn it was to get up and put wood on the fire in the middle of the night. Now we know, it's always his turn, because I won't do it.

One thing we always had a big difference of opinion on was how I should drive. Mainly he would tell me how to drive and I would get mad.

These days he still tells me how to drive and I still get mad, but I guess there are some things that you just can't reach a consensus on. But at least we concede that we can't, so we have that in common...

The Terminology of Ranching

Having been a rancher's wife now for more than 20 years I'd almost forgotten what it feels like to be a city slicker and not know the difference between heifers, cows, steers and bulls. I can remember calling them all "cows" regardless of their gender, size or disposition.

Disposition, I've found, is a valuable key to determining the sex of cattle without having to peek at their undercarriage. If you see one that looks mad, you can be sure it's a cow. If you see one that looks a little irritated, it is more than likely a heifer on her way to becoming a cow.

A bovine (cattle genus) that stands around staring at the other cows with a gleam in its eyes is more than likely a bull. However, one that doesn't seem to know where it's going or what to do is a steer, they always appear a little confused, especially about their gender.

I've also discovered that steers aren't the only ones that have horns. Hereford isn't a mispronunciation of heifer. And calves, although cute, can kick and head butt really hard, and they don't care if it hurts your feelings.

I have run into quite a few other confusing ranching terminologies on the ranch over the years so I will attempt to clear up a few of them in order to save you city slickers from embarrassment:

A saddle iron is not used to get the wrinkles out of saddles; it is a branding iron that can be carried on a saddle.

Shelly cows are not cows that all have the same name; they are older cows in poor condition.

A cow waddle has nothing to do with the way a cow walks, it's a method of making the skin under the neck of cattle hang down to help identify them.

A steer, contrary to his name, usually does not have any special navigation skills; it's a castrated bovine.

Commercial producers do not film deodorant ads for TV; they raise cattle to sell to other ranchers.

Polled cattle have not been given the option of stating their opinion; they are a naturally hornless breed.

Cow chips are not a crisp, salty snack made from beef, they are dried cow poop and not meant for human consumption.

Dorks and dinks — most city slickers don't have problems with theses terms because calves that are dorks and dinks really are the human equivalent of those words. So far ranchers haven't caught on to using the word "nerd" yet though.

Cow-hocked doesn't mean a cow has been taken to a pawnshop, in fact it has nothing to do with cows. It is a term used to describe a horse's hind legs that almost touch at the hocks (knees).

A sucker has nothing to do with candy on a stick; it is a baby pig before weaning.

Gilt has nothing to do with the way you feel after doing something bad; it is a young female pig.

Barrow has nothing to do with asking your neighbor to loan you something, nor is it a one-wheeled manure hauler (as in wheelbarrow), it is a pig that has been castrated before puberty.

A hand isn't something you scratch or applaud with; it is a term used to measure how tall a horse is. Must have been before they had tape measures...

Driving horses —this one is confusing because horses don't actually drive; however, they can be driven.

If someone asks you for tack, you shouldn't go get a pushpin. Tack is used to describe horse equipment, why... we'll never know.

A hotshot isn't someone who thinks they're really cool, it's an instrument used to poke cattle in the butt when they won't move. Many ranchers try to use it on their wives too, but usually find they don't get the desired results.

Chute isn't something that happens when you fire a gun, it's a device used to hold livestock so they can be given vaccines. Helpful hint: don't ever let your husband talk you into putting your head in the head catch of a chute to see if it works.

A hooker is not a woman of ill repute; it is a bull that uses its horns to hook a rider off its back in a rodeo. So if your husband tells you he rode a hooker, don't get excited.

If someone asks you to eat Rocky Mountain oysters, don't do it! They are not seafood; I repeat, they are not seafood.

Same goes for son-of-a-bitch stew unless you have a hankering for calf brains and thymus glands.

A hay burner isn't someone who goes around setting hay stacks on fire, it's what ranchers call a horse that is not doing much other than standing around eating all day— much like a teenager.

When someone asks you how many head you have, it is impolite to say "I have one head on top of my neck, how many head do you have?" Head refers to the number of animal units.

A broke horse is not one that is busted, it is one that has been trained to let someone ride on its back.

A stud usually refers to a male horse that has not been castrated, but ranchers often use it when referring to themselves.

These are just a few of the terms ranchers use that I have learned the definitions of over the years. When a rancher uses them in complete sentences though sometimes I still have a hard time figuring out what they are talking about:

"I took that cow waddled Shelly and the two dorks to the sale and picked up a hooker and a little gilt. I hotshoted the hooker through the chute first to get a look at its Rocky Mountain oysters. I had a son-of-a-bitch stew and bought a broke 15-hand hay burner that could drive. I really wanted to get a sucker, but they didn't have one so I decided on a barrow... Ain't I the stud?"

And they think the hip-hop lingo that our teenagers use is hard to understand....

A New Generation

I was disheartened recently to discover that I'm too young to be a Baby Boomer and too old to be a Generation X'er. I bemoaned the fact that I had no generation term to describe myself. I felt like a generational misfit, a rancher's wife with no age bracket other than "past her prime."

My husband always thought I was among the Generation X'ers because X'ers are known for their casual approach to authority. He says my approach to his authority is definitely too casual!

I always figured I was a Baby Boomer because they are known for being adaptive, and as most ranchers' wives know, it takes a lot of adapting to live with a rancher.

But, since I don't remember the Burma Shave signs of the Boomer era and Generation X'ers have no idea who Beaver Cleaver and Barbie's friend Midge are, I did the only thing I could. I Googled to find out if I have a generation. And to my surprise, I do. I am of the birth era dubbed "Generation Jones." Or as I found we like to call ourselves "Jonesers."

The term Joneser comes from the idea of "conspicuous consumption." Frankly, I would rather my consumption was inconspicuous, but I guess that's the price I pay for being of this generation.

The information I found stated that Generation Jones is largely an anonymous generation — no wonder I didn't know what generation I belong to. We're so anonymous, we don't even know who we are.

Apparently Jonesers are also considered the "lost generation." Once again, this explains why I didn't know, and perhaps why I need a GPS when I go mushrooming.

The Internet confirmed that I had huge expectations as a child in the 1960s, and then was confronted with a different reality when I came of age in the 1970s. Fortunately, I decided that I could still be a Joneser, even if I never came of age. I nearly came of age a few times, but it didn't take.

We are also often referred to as the "Tweeners" — stuck in the middle between the Baby Boomers and the Generation X'ers. And, we are known as the "computer pioneers."

Apparently, with our computer backgrounds, you will find a lot of us Tweeners tweeting on Twitter, the Internet social site. Facebook, another popular Internet site, also has special sections for Jonesers, but it's not as fun to say as Twitter.

Some say Jonesers are always jonsing (craving or yearning) for something better. Can you blame us? In our teenage years we drove AMC Gremlins and Ford Pintos, for crying out loud.

Even though I have finally solved my generational identity crisis, I have decided I would rather start a new generation for those of us who are in between the Boomers and X'ers and don't quite feel like keeping up with the Joneses. I call it Generation Rancher (GR).

The neat thing about Generation Ranchers is that they can be any age; it doesn't matter what time frame they were born in. They just have to like cows.

Generation Ranchers are known for persevering in tough economic times by utilizing baling twine and duct tape for equipment repairs, and pretty much everything else.

GR husbands like to give their wives instructions, over and over again, just in case we have a dirt clod in our ears and missed it the first, second or third time.

GR's emphasize teamwork. Ranching husbands are part of the team and their wives do the work.

GR husbands are born knowing how to rake hay and harrow fields, dig postholes and fix fences, but since it's their nature to be generous, they give these responsibilities to their wives.

Since they are also goal-oriented, GR husbands often times make it their goal to teach their wives how to properly back up a vehicle. Ironically, they must never reach their goal because this training takes place about a bazillions times a year.

GR wives are lovely, youthful no matter what age they are, highly intelligent, wonderful spouses and mothers, and basically perfect. This is the advantage of being the inventor of a new generation term; I can give us any characteristics I want!

Unlike Generation Jonesers, Generation Ranchers aren't typically known for being "trendy," but someday maybe Levis stained with tractor oil and feed store hats will make it into mainstream fashion. It happened with bellbottoms, which are simply hand-me-down pants that are too big, and platform shoes.

Not many people know this, but platform shoes were invented by ranchers to keep from getting cow poop on their bellbottoms. And this happened before we even knew we had a generation term. Now that we know we are Generation Ranchers, I'm sure we will be coming up with many more clever ideas like how to keep cow poop off of our shoes....

"*Good is when I steal other people's wives and cattle; bad is when they steal mine.*"
          Hottentot proverb

Caution, Driving with a Husband May Be Hazardous

I learned how to drive when I was about 13. My Dad took me out to a flat dirt field in the country in an older jeep and taught me how to shift gears without popping the clutch and killing the engine.

Later my mom taught me the finer art of parallel parking and maneuvering in traffic. Unfortunately I had to figure out how to put on makeup in the rear-view mirror while driving on my own.

My brother, who is almost two years older, taught me how to peel out and spin cookies. (Oops! Sorry, I wasn't supposed to tell mom that!)

By the time I was in college, I was driving long distance road trips in all kinds of conditions including black ice, snow and fog, most of the time with a carload of noisy friends.

Nowadays I put about 20,000 miles a year in the driver's seat in our car, pickup, jeep and tractors combined. Sometimes I have to share my seat with the dog, but I think it's accurate to say I do most of the driving.

All of this isn't too unusual, but I had thought with this experience it would be safe to assume that I know how to drive. But apparently all of that early training and subsequent decades of driving is not sufficient, because my husband continues to give me instruction on an almost daily basis.

Several years ago when he decided that I should be the designated driver when we go places, I thought, "Wow, he must really think I'm a good driver!" Turns out he thought it would just be easier to tell me how to drive if he were in the passenger seat. Why he has decided to make it his primary goal in life to make me a better driver remains a mystery.

Even though I have been driving sticks for the better part of 30 years, and somehow manage to get where I am going without having the transmission fall out, apparently, according to him, I really don't know how to shift.

From his observations, he tells me I am either riding the clutch, holding it in too long, letting it out too fast or using the wrong part of my foot. I swear he must have a security camera on the floor by my left foot; otherwise, how can he see what's going on down there that well from the passenger seat? I just know that one of these days I'll be on the Internet at YouTube looking at funny cow videos and a video called "Debby Has Her Foot on the Clutch" will appear.

And then there is the stick itself. Apparently I operate it with all of the finesse of someone trying to cram a wet noodle through the eye of a needle. I should shift faster. I should shift slower. I should have shifted up when I shifted down, and down when I shifted up. I shift at the wrong time or I shift at the right time, and then it's back to the whole foot on the clutch thing.

He tells me to listen to the RPMs so I will know when to shift. I tell him to listen to the car door slam so he will know when I get out.

And this all takes place before I even get out of the driveway!

Once we're on the open road, I drive the speed limit and he says I drive too slow. He tells me I will get a ticket for impeding traffic, so I speed up. When he's not looking at the speedometer, I slow down again because I don't want to get a ticket for speeding.

With all of this speeding up and slowing down, I'm thinking of installing hazard warnings on my car — flashing yellow lights and a sign that reads "Caution, speed fluctuates due to nagging husband." Oops, sorry, he says he doesn't nag, he is just trying to help. "Caution, speed fluctuates due to husband trying to help."

Maybe I would be better off to get one of those window suction cup signs that says, "Husband on Board." That would probably clue most people in to what is going on....

Once we get into town is when the real fun begins!

Apparently I wait too long for cars to pass before I pull out into the street. After all if we could have trimmed three seconds off of that wait, we'd get home three seconds sooner.

He also says I'm always taking corners too close or too fast. Most women get excited if they get a new job with a big fat raise, someone gives them diamonds or they have a baby. If I could turn a corner at the right angle and velocity it would be right up there with that kind of thrill.

Backing up and parallel parking – let's not even go there! Many married couples have divorced over far less strenuous situations.

And parking lots are like kryptonite to Superman — they are best avoided. If Obama can win the Nobel Peace Prize, I should be able to get one for finding the right place to park in a parking lot — that is if I ever do.

Traffic lights, stop signs and pedestrians are always getting in our way of making good time. Making good time appears to be right at the top of the list of important things to accomplish, just above saving the planet.

Either I stop at the lights or for pedestrians for too long, or don't even need to stop in the first place. I'm wondering if we could call the local police and have them clear the way for us when we come to town.

"Yes, this is Debby Schoeningh, I'm coming to town with my husband. Can you please time it so all of the lights are green when we go through and not allow anyone to cross the street during our visit? Also, please notify all available units that we need to make good time."

Police dispatch would immediately radio their officers, "Schoeningh is coming to town again and she has her husband with her. If you want that Christmas bonus you better make sure they are in and out of town in less than 30 minutes. And disregard any traffic violations; her husband is still teaching her how to drive."

When the Department of Motor Vehicles teach about driving hazards, they forget to mention the dangers of having your husband with you....

"What?" Hang on a second; my husband is looking over my shoulder as I write this. He says he thinks I may be exaggerating.

"Well, maybe I am, a little...."

About The Author

Debby Schoeningh and her husband, Mike, live at the base of the Elkhorn Mountains in rural Eastern Oregon where they have a cow/calf operation.

Her writing and photography have appeared in the *Western Horseman* magazine, the *Oregon Business Magazine* and the *Cascade Cattleman*. She continues to contribute to several publications on a regular basis including the *Ruralite* magazine and the Capital Press newspaper. She is also a writer/editor at *The Record-Courier* newspaper where she writes her column "The Country Side." "Cattle Drive" is her third book.

Debby enjoys the beauty of nature and spends her spare time photographing the ranching life and Eastern Oregon's landscape. Her work can be seen on the Internet at http://www.thecountrysidepress.com.

The End

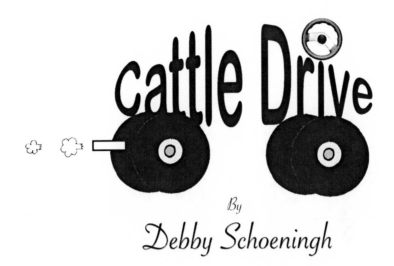

By

Debby Schoeningh

Published by

www.thecountrysidepress.com

Other books by Debby Schoeningh
"Tails From The Country Side"
"The Horseless Rancher"

The Country Side Press books are available at your local bookstore or various Internet sites including Amazon.com

Visit Debby at

www.myspace.com/thecountrysidepress

FaceBook